THE MONEY COMPASS

AN INSIDER'S GUIDE TO FINANCIAL SUCCESS

HOW TO TAKE CONTROL OF YOUR FINANCES AND LIVE THE FUTURE YOU WANT

Written by
JULIE HUNT

authors
AND CO.

CONTENTS

MEET JULIE HUNT

Julie has over 20 years' experience working in the financial service industry and has lots of letters after her name and certificates to prove it. For the past 17 years, she's been running Face to Face Finance, a successful Independent Financial Advice firm based in Norfolk, UK.

As the owner of multiple businesses herself, Julie comes into contact with countless other women in business; women with busy lives and lots of priorities, and she wants to help by equipping them with simple tools and the support needed to make continued progress towards their financial goals. She set up The Money Compass to do just that, enabling Julie to add podcast host and owner of a thriving Facebook group to her list of accomplishments.

Globetrotting Julie loves nothing more than to visit far-flung places. It's a good job that she's organised with money because, despite all the weird and wonderful places she's been, a trip to Las Vegas with her husband remains a firm favourite!

Connect with Julie:

https://www.facebook.com/groups/the-money-compass

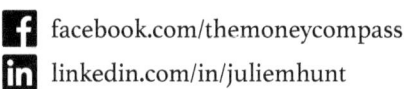 facebook.com/themoneycompass
linkedin.com/in/juliemhunt

This book is dedicated to Ralph for all his love and patience, and always believing in me

ACKNOWLEDGEMENTS

Special thanks to the awesome team at Face to Face Finance who put up with me on a daily basis. Thanks to Becky and Emma for their feedback.

And finally, a massive thank you to Emma Raines for all her feedback, support and great ideas. I couldn't have done it without you.

INTRODUCTION

After over 20 years working in the financial services industry, I have found that many books about money just aren't that readable and are predominately aimed at the male market. Although the dark ages have been and gone, there is still a feeling from many that men look after the money, and women follow behind. Now, I know that this is no longer the case but far too often have I spoken to fellow female business owners who are well respected within their respective industries yet, when it comes to their own finances, they feel somewhat intimidated.

Having worked in the male dominated financial services industry for such an extensive period, it is a sad truth that the world of money is still one where men rule the roost. When I walk into any industry event, I am predominately surrounded by older men and only a small handful of women. If this is what it is like within the industry itself, it's little wonder that on the outside, many women are still shying away from dealing with money.

Simply sticking your head in the sand won't make any financial concerns go away, nor will it magically make a money tree start growing in your back garden. Like everything else in life, your finances need your attention to help nurture and improve them. If you know you need to save more money for that new car, why wait three years until your current car is on its last legs before you make a start? What's stopping you from starting to save a little each month now towards that new car to help take the pressure off later down the line? To quote US personal finance celebrity Dave Ramsey, "you must gain control over your money – or the lack of it will forever control you".

Lack of confidence and experience in being actively involved in this area is often to blame and that's something that I hope to address within the coming chapters.

BREAKING TABOOS

In the years I have worked in financial services, I have found "why" to be the most powerful of words.

Why don't we talk about money? Why is money important? Why are we jealous of other people's money? Why does money matter?

Have you ever noticed that when you're out with friends, perhaps enjoying a meal, it's very rare that money comes up? It's not on the casual conversation taboo list, like religion and politics, but it feels a bit like someone added it to the taboo list when we weren't looking!

I get that we don't like to talk about how much we earn - we are British after all - but what's the best bank account out there? Where do you save your money? What budgeting tips work for you? – how often do these topics come up?

Not very often, for most people. I'm used to talking about money in my day to day working life, but out for drinks? It has taken a lot of years for those kinds of conversations to feel comfortable. I've had people walk away from me at events when I have told them what I do for a living, or they have simply stated what they have done financially and asked for reassurance. I'm not sure if they expect me to ask for a copy of their bank and portfolio statement there and then, but the thought of talking about money is an uncomfortable one for many people!

This book is my mission to take money off the taboo list – it will make "why" your most powerful ally, rather than an embarrassing question.

WHY A BOOK ABOUT MONEY?

I believe that all women should be responsible for their finances, and I want to help female business owners to become more financially organised, have peace of mind and feel prepared for the rest of their lives, through educating and empowering them with financial guidance and advice.

This book is designed to help with just that. By providing you with knowledge and understanding, your confidence will grow. Your money and finances will no longer be a scary topic that you try and avoid at all costs, or one that you keep putting off because you just can't find the time. The more you read and talk about finance, the easier it will become.

Each chapter has been designed to give you take away pointers and actions to help you become more financially confident and organised, giving you a sense of control over what the next steps are for you.

I'm not claiming to be the oracle of all things finance (although 20 years in the industry puts me a fair few steps ahead of most!), however I do firmly believe that by sharing my knowledge and experiences with you, I can put you in good stead for your financial future. Much of what I have learned along the way hasn't come from text books and study guides, but from the situations and scenarios which my clients have found themselves in. Whether it's been about their retirement planning - *"how much will I need to save if I want to retire on £2,000 per month at 60?"*, their investments and savings - *"how can I save enough money to fund my children's education"* and even *"should I invest or pay off the mortgage?"* – there really is no such thing as a silly question, and if there was, I guarantee I will have already been asked it!

I promise you that you already know more than you think you do when it comes to money. When reading this book, I hope you surprise yourself and even pat yourself on the back when you think "yes, I know that already". I hope that gives you the confidence to read on.

When I sat down to write the introduction for this book, it was a Saturday in January, I was in the dining room watching what seemed like hundreds of small garden birds flying to the bird feeders, taking a small piece of food and flying away to eat it, before flying back for another piece. I realised that's what I want this book to be about for you, dear reader.

Don't worry, I don't expect you to grow wings and start flying round the garden! But I want you to feel that you can fly into the book, read the chapter you need, consume and absorb the information, then fly back in again as and when you need.

I have broken the book down into different topics and bite size chapters to make it as reader friendly as possible, meaning you can simply read up on a topic that catches your eye, or you can read it from cover to cover. I have created a workbook which you can download from The Money Compass website, and complete as you work your way through the book. I know from personal experience that I'm a cover-to-cover kind of girl! But please go at your own pace and enjoy the experience.

MONEY MINDSET

Before we delve into looking at the nitty gritty of your finances, it's important to make sure your Money Mindset is in the right place. Let's look at how to do just that, and what that right place looks like for you.

First things first, what is Money Mindset?

Mindset is an established set of attitudes held by someone. Money Mindset is essentially your belief and attitudes towards your finances.

A positive money mindset is where you have the freedom to spend or not to spend, you don't compare yourself to others and are happy with your situation.

A negative money mindset is where you feel you will never have enough money, you don't deserve that money, you will self-sabotage at every chance, and compare yourself with others.

Some people might describe their Money Mindsets with phrases such as having an abundance mindset or a scarcity mindset. A person with an abundance mindset believes that there is plenty out there for everyone. By someone earning more than them, it doesn't limit the amount of money that they can earn. They also feel responsible for the money they bring in - they don't believe that it's anyone else's responsibility.

Someone with a scarcity mindset believes the opposite. They feel that there is never enough to go round. They feel that it is someone else's responsibility to give them more money, be that their employer, their partner, or other people in their life.

WHERE DOES YOUR MONEY MINDSET COME FROM?

Our Money Mindset comes from our past experiences with money, how money was treated and addressed when we were growing up, the beliefs about money of the people around us and the thoughts we expose ourselves to. A lot of this comes from our childhood.

It is said that by the age of seven your Money Mindset will be set, which means that those people around us at that young age will have instilled the messages you hear in your head throughout your life when you are dealing with money. That's pretty incredible.

Think back to your earliest memory of money, this will start giving you an idea of what your money mindset is.

My earliest memory of money is my dad coming home with his pay packet in cash and giving it to my mum. She then took this into the bedroom and counted the money into envelopes, labelled them with things like electricity - £3, holidays - £2, Christmas - £2, coal – £2, and putting the envelopes in a black and red tin in the bedroom drawer. We didn't have much money, but my mum was very good at managing it to make sure we still had a nice Christmas and holidays.

I also remember that my brother and I were given pocket money. We would get 10p a week for our age, so 50p at 5, 60p at 6 and so on. The tooth fairy would also visit us bringing 10p for a small tooth and 20p for the big ones!

However, I didn't realise we were poor when I was growing up, it was only when I was an adult that I heard the story of my parents buying their house. Back then, you needed three months of wage slips to get a mortgage, and my dad got a job working a campaign at the local sugar beet factory. The work campaign lasted three months so, as they bought the house, my dad was left without a job. My mum used to pack fireworks in the evenings at home for extra money to ensure they could keep up repayments.

My parents took a lot of risk by signing up for a mortgage not knowing how they were going to make the monthly payments. Neither of them came from a background where they would be able to borrow money, but they believed that the universe would provide the opportunities they needed to meet those repayments. I'm pretty sure the term "Abundant Mindset" wasn't about when they were 20, but if it was, that would definitely be what they had. They knew that if they worked hard, everything would work out in the end. I think that a lot of my positive Money Mindset comes from my parents.

I believe that money has a part to play in all our lives. It gives us freedom that we wouldn't have without money. I believe that if you work hard enough, and want something badly enough, then it will all work out right in the end. Thinking positive will ensure everything turns out positively! But, and this is an important point, thinking positively isn't enough on its own – you need to take positive action too!

Anyway, that's enough about me, let's talk about you. What is your money mindset?

Understanding where your money mindset comes from is the best first step to working out what your money mindset is.

It's time to get all that information down on paper (or typed up - whichever you prefer) and spend some time thinking about what your money mindset is. What phrases do you hear yourself thinking or saying? Here are some common ones you may recognise from your childhood:

- Money doesn't grow on trees
- I'm not made of money
- You have to work hard to make money
- Money is the root of all evil
- Rich people are greedy
- Money can't buy happiness.

Think about what your views are on the following questions and what these questions bring up for you. Write down your answers.

What is your view on earning money?

Do you think it's important to earn lots of money? Do you see it as a means to an end? How do you feel about the money you earn?

What do you believe about saving and having money?

Does having savings make you feel happy? Or do you feel that it's lost money that you could be spending on something now?

How do you feel about debt?

Do you see debt as a good thing or a bad thing? Does it keep you awake at night worrying about it?

How do you feel about paying off debt?

Do you feel relieved, a weight lifted? Or are you indifferent to clearing your debts?

How do you feel about spending money?

Does spending money make you feel guilty? Do you love spending money?

How do you feel after spending money?

Does it bring you joy initially, then regret later? Or do you not give it a second thought?

What is your opinion of "rich people"?

Do you have an opinion on this or do you see all people as the same? Do you see rich people as boastful show-offs? Do you feel that if people aren't rich, then they are not as important because they have less?

How do you feel about receiving money?

Do you feel you don't deserve the money, that you're not worthy? Or are you ready to receive with open arms?

Once you have written down your thoughts on these money questions, the next step is to grab a couple of different colour highlighter pens. Go through each of the views you have written down and highlight positive comments in one colour, and negative comments in a different colour.

Please don't worry if you're not sure whether something is positive or negative, and definitely do not worry if you have more negative comments than positive ones.

After this exercise, read through the positive comments you have highlighted and the negative comments you have highlighted. This will help you see what your thoughts are on different money scenarios. You will be able to see where your mindset is predominately positive, and also where you have a more negative mindset. This should help give you an idea of your overall current Money Mindset.

Some examples of positive and negative money mindsets to each question are below:

What is your view on earning money?

"I think it's important to have lots of money, but you must take time to enjoy it."

"I will never earn any more money as I don't deserve more."

What do you believe about saving and having money?

"I feel it's important to have savings and there is usually something I'm saving for such as a car or a deposit for a house."

"I don't have enough money to save."

How do you feel about debt?

"There are good debts like having a mortgage, but bad debt is bad. If I can't afford it, I won't have it."

"I am burdened with lots of debt, and can't see a way forward."

How do you feel about paying off debt?

"I feel much better knowing I have very little debt than I did when I had a lot of debt."

"I can't think about paying off debt. I can't see that ever happening."

How do you feel about spending money?

"I enjoy spending as long as I have the money to spend."

"I spend to forget my debts."

How do you feel after spending money?

"Spending money on physical things and going out brings me joy."

"I regret most of my purchases."

What is your opinion of "rich people"?

"I'm very jealous of rich people."

How do you feel about receiving money?

"If I have worked for the money then I will receive with open arms."

"If it was gifted, I feel guilty."

Now we need to look at ways of overcoming any negative Money Mindsets.

WHAT ARE MONEY BLOCKS?

I was out for a walk with a friend, and the conversation came round to flying, and flying first class. My friend turned around and said "I'll never be able to afford to fly first class"! That is a money block right there – if you don't think you will ever to be able to do something the likelihood is that you won't.

Another very common one is "I'm no good with money". You're already telling yourself that you will always make poor decisions with money.

I once had a friend who always complained "it's not my responsibility" – it's not their fault they had no money, it's X or Y's fault! Our relationship came to an end when she told me it was alright for me, I could afford to give her money as I had just had a big holiday. It wasn't her fault she had spent her money on cigarettes and Sky, and couldn't afford to feed her children...

When it comes to business, some of the common money blocks are related to success and comparing yourself to others – that other person is better than you and you will never be as successful. However, we are all on our own individual journeys – by comparing to others, we have forgotten to concentrate on our own success.

Another big one in business is a limiting belief in the amount of money you can earn. I have seen people with an upper limit in their mind, and they struggle to earn more than this amount.

Look through your negative highlighted comments. How many of these are stopping you from realising your full potential when it comes to money?

OTHER PEOPLE AND YOUR MONEY MINDSET

The more you look through your comments on your views about money, the more things will jump out at you. You might also start noticing things that your friends say to you and noticing what their money mindset is too!

Are you surrounding yourself with negative minded people? Are their views rubbing off on you? Do they think that you will fail?

Have a serious look around you. Is your team thrumming with positivity for what you are looking to achieve, or are they just waiting for you fail? Listen to what you say, and what others around you are saying, and remember it's not always true!

A client was recently telling me all about her new house, which she was very excited about. She told me "I told everyone that we had downsized, but actually, it's bigger!"

She was worried about other people's perception of the new house. Rather than celebrating her lovely new home, she was diminishing the achievement.

I know I have been guilty of similar in the past. When I bought my new car a year ago, when anyone saw it, I regaled them with the tale of how it was X amount cheaper than it should have been – as I somehow had to justify the purchase, rather than saying – thank you, I love it!! Which of course I do!

It can be interesting to take a moment to consider how other people influence your Money Mindset and factor that in too.

CHANGING YOUR MONEY MINDSET

Having the right Money Mindset is really important when we start looking at your financial goals. If your Money Mindset is predominantly negative, if you feel that you will never be able to buy a house, you will never earn more money than you currently do, etc., then you will limit yourself with the goals that you think you will be able to achieve.

Secretly, you may covet a bigger house, a new Mercedes and having a work life balance where you holiday to exotic places four or five times a year, and work three days a week. But if your mindset is telling you that you're not good enough or worthy of having these things, then the chances of you achieving them are so much lower. If your mindset is positive, and you believe everything is possible if you work smarter, you'll be able to set realistic goals which will stepping stone to your bigger goals and know that, one day, that will be your life.

If you have a super positive Money Mindset already, that is brilliant, but if you feel that your Money Mindset has some negative elements, what can you do to change it?

The first step is to be aware that there isn't a quick fix to changing your Money Mindset. I wish I could tell you there is, but unfortunately not.

All of the work in this chapter will help you establish what your Money Mindset is, whether those views are positive or negative, and what triggers your negative or positive views on Money Mindset.

Just being aware of the negative elements will have a massive impact on your Money Mindset. If you can accept your views, and acknowledge the negative views, you can turn those negative thoughts into more positive ones – if you don't realise your views are negative, then you won't know that you need to make any changes! But once you become aware, then it means you are on the right track to do something about it.

Personally, I find keeping a journal of my money experiences each day and categorising them as either a negative or positive money mindset has really helped me recognise patterns of behaviour, and now when I feel a negative thought popping into my head, I can recognise it for what it is, and change my negative thoughts into a positive thought.

You will be surprised when you start looking for them, there will be lots of things that pop up. As your awareness grows, you can start taking steps to address them.

Having positive affirmations around Money Mindset can also really help. Looking back at your Money Mindset journal entries from the day before will show you areas where you have struggled.

For example, a potential client queried your price; at the time you felt perhaps they were right, your prices were too high, you weren't worth what you were charging. You doubted yourself.

What could help you overcome this negative thought in the future? Try telling yourself every morning that you are worthy of your prices; you deserve to earn what you charge. Write it in your journal, repeat it out loud. I have a friend who writes their affirmation in lipstick on the mirror in their bathroom!

Here are a few ideas for affirmations:

I know what I am doing

I am worthy of financial stability

I am worth the money

Find an affirmation that you feel comfortable with, even create your own. Remember, if you don't feel comfortable with what you are saying, then it just won't work.

Journaling and affirmations are a great start, but this is something you need to be thinking about all the time you are making decisions about money, spending money, and even when other people are spending money (or not). Your thoughts around all these areas will help shape your future Money Mindset.

WHAT YOU KNOW NOW:

- What Money Mindset is
- The difference between a positive and a negative mindset
- How to recognise different types of mindset
- Where your Money Mindset comes from
- What money blocks are and how to overcome them.

2

RELATIONSHIPS AND MONEY

We've looked at your Money Mindset, now it's time to delve a bit deeper into your relationship with Money, not just with yourself but, if you have one, with your partner in life. This can apply to a business partner as well a life partner.

Do you think you have a healthy relationship with money? When you have money does it burn a hole in your pocket? Or are you a regular saver?

Does money make you feel more confident or less secure? Have you made good financial decisions in the past? Are you nervous about making decisions – do you ask for advice from a partner, a family member or a friend before making a financial decision?

It's great to ask for advice but don't fall into the trap of asking too many people, as you may get more answers than you know what to do with.

If you ask someone and you already know what they are going to say, why did you ask them? Are you after affirmation it's the right decision, or are you punishing yourself as you know that they would say no?

Recently, someone I know received some money after the death of a close family member, with the specific instructions it wasn't to be wasted on a new car – as they already had a perfectly good car. So why, six months later, did they go to the partner of the deceased person to ask their opinion on buying a new car with that money?

I find that nine times out of ten, deep down we already know whether we should make that purchase or not!

IMPULSIVE SPENDING

Online shopping and television shopping channels make it easier to make purchases if you are an impulsive shopper. Buyer's regret is a big thing, but how many times do the items bought actually get returned? Or do they end up with the labels still on in the bottom of the wardrobe or the cupboard, and end up in the bin or the charity shop bag 12 months later?

If you know you are an impulsive shopper, then doing something to curb your habit is a good place to start when it comes to improving your financial situation.

I have a bit of an Amazon addiction, especially with DVDs and books. I set up an AmazonSmile account to support my favourite charity, however the Smile feature doesn't work on the Amazon app, therefore I have to order through the website to ensure the donation is made.

This is a great deterrent! I can add items into my Amazon basket when doing a bit of browsing on the app, then the next morning, I pop on to the computer and check what I've been thinking about ordering. It gives me an opportunity to question whether I really *need* that movie in my life and do some serious basket editing before I press the buy button. It's certainly saved me from some films with dodgy reviews which seemed like a good idea when I was watching the trailer!

The same principle can be used with any online shopping - pop the item in your basket, and sleep on it. You'll be surprised how many times you decide that the "sale" item or top you thought you ready needed the night before ends up being forgotten!

IMPULSIVE SAVING

The opposite to impulsive spending is impulsive saving – you save every penny and then plead poverty whenever you are invited out, as you quietly accumulate your wealth. Remember, it's probably not your life's ambition to be the richest person in the graveyard!

With spending and saving there is a balancing act to achieve what you want to achieve, and enjoy life while you do it.

RELATIONSHIPS

Money is the number one issue that couples fight about.

It's not that hard to believe. Before you got together, you were both doing your own thing when it comes to money. You have your own relationship with money, and suddenly there is another person and their relationship with money joining the mix.

Personally, I think it's important to start talking about money with your partner before you take any big commitment steps like moving in together. This way, any differences in opinion when it comes to money can be bought into the light and discussed before you get yourself into a situation that's a lot harder to get out of!

A client of mine recently split from her partner; she was young going into the relationship and money wasn't really discussed. It was only when they were living together that it became apparent they had completely different mindsets towards money. Whilst she was a saver and wanted to save up to make a purchase, he was very much "I want it now, that's what credit cards and credit are for". So, a new settee would go on credit, rather than saving the money to buy it.

In the end, the relationship broke down, with the differing approaches to money being a major factor in the breakup.

I'm not saying that a spender and a saver can't live happily together, but making sure that there is communication upfront about how that will work is really important.

One solution to this can be having a joint bank account where you both pay in a set amount each month, and this account pays all the joint bills, such as the mortgage, insurances and utilities. Then you both manage your own separate bank accounts for the rest of your money and do with it as you wish.

A colleague of mine was a saver. Her partner was a spender, always out drinking with his friends, while she saved her money to go on holiday to amazing locations. And she did just that – she would go away with friends, and leave her partner at home!

I remember meeting a couple in China when I was back-packing and, chatting to the wife, she told me that she had been in a relationship similar to my colleague's. Her partner wasn't interested in travelling or saving to do things, and she would travel alone. Eventually for her, the relationship broke down – she was having the most amazing experiences but wasn't coming home at night to the person who she had shared them with, and she wanted to be able to share those experiences with the person she was meant to be spending her life with.

I think the above scenarios demonstrate that there are different ways to approach tricky financial situations, and what works for one person won't necessarily work for another. In my opinion, communication is the key.

In my relationship, we are both savers, although I think my husband might say I like to spend – especially when it comes to my haircut!

DEBT AND RELATIONSHIPS

We've looked at saving and spending in relationships, but another area which can be very emotive is debt. This can certainly be the cause of a lot of friction within a relationship.

I know of someone who found out on her wedding night that her new husband had taken out loans in her name to pay off his gambling debts! I can't imagine how she felt, or how she didn't get up and walk out. Love can be a strange beast. But this couple are far from alone…

According to research in America, 1 in 3 people have hidden purchases from their partners![1]

It may not seem like a big deal, but let's call it by its other name, financial infidelity – it suddenly feels a lot more serious!

Why do it? We may have seen our parents hiding purchases from each other as we grew up: "sshh, don't tell your mum/dad about buying you x, y or z". It all goes back to learnt behaviour from our childhoods.

It could be because of the reaction we anticipate from our partner – how will they react if you have spent money on a new pair of shoes? Recently, my favourite dark brown knee boots fell apart. Aside from the departure of my favourite boots, I knew replacing them was going to be a right pain. However, a friend had recommended Fairfax and Favor – and those boots did look lovely! However, being a big believer in owning your purchases, and not hiding them from your partner, I was quite shocked to see that there is an option when you go to place the order to "Add an Alibi".

By adding an alibi, the company will enclose a note within your order, and you can select whether you go for the "purchase" as a competition win or a free gift, so that your partner won't realise (unless they see your bank statement or credit card bill) that you have paid for them.

None of this helps us to have a healthy relationship with our partners.

I believe the key to all relationship and money issues is answered with one word, COMMUNICATION!

A WORD ON MORTGAGES

Nowadays, getting a mortgage together is a commitment almost as big as getting married for some couples. You are signing a 25-year contract (sometimes longer) with a person – it doesn't get much more serious than that!

What do you know about that person? Sure, the mortgage lender will have run a credit score on you both, but what does tell you about each other's habits?

I once helped a couple get a mortgage where the finances were insanely tight. One half of the couple was a saver; she was frugal with her spending. On the other hand, her partner spent money frivolously and was in a small amount of debt, but the house was their dream. Once they had moved in, he wished to express his thanks to me with flowers and champagne when a thank you would suffice.

I'm pleased to report that fifteen years later, they are still living happily together and have upgraded their property in recent years. However, in the early days they had to learn to communicate with each other. They set up separate accounts, one for the mortgage and the bills, which they both input into, and a separate savings account for joint goals. Finally, they both then had an account for their personal outgoings, which they could spend as they wished.

In the early years, she always had money for nights out with friends, whereas he would sometimes end up with no money left at the end of the month. Gradually, over time, he learnt new saving and spending habits, which meant that they both enjoyed going out.

If you opt for a joint account with your partner for bills, you will need to sit down and agree how to work out the amount to pay into that account each month. What if one of you earns a lot more than the other? Does a set split of 50/50 work, or if one of you is earning 25% more than the other, should the higher earner contribute more to the account? There's no right answer to this, but it is important you agree.

TINY FEET

Imagine, it's all going swimmingly, you have resolved any differences you have regarding money, you agree on debt, and the bank accounts are all sorted. It's time for the next stage of the journey for many – children.

Alongside all the other changes that come with having children – the sudden responsibility of a new life, sleepless nights, how to make ends meet with a reduction in income – you also need to consider your views on spending money on your child.

This may once again stem back to your childhoods. You didn't have much so you want to make sure your child wants for nothing? Or, you didn't have much, but it didn't do you any harm?

As your child grows up, will you be a united front, or will your child always be able to play one of you off against the other? Sitting down before it gets to that stage is really important so that, if your views do differ greatly, you can have a compromise in place that you are both happy with before it becomes a real issue.

Don't forget, your Money Mindset often stems from your childhood. What do you want your child's Money Mindset to be?

It all seems like a lot to think about, but the better you know yourself and your habits, the easier it will be to add extra people into the equation.

Remember: with any relationship there is always compromise, whether that is with yourself or with someone else, and there are people out there who can help you with these areas if you need it.

WHAT YOU KNOW NOW:

- Communication is the key to dealing with money issues in a relationship;
- Make sure you have the money conversation before making any big financial commitments together;
- A spender and a saver can live together in harmony, as long as there is a big dose of communication and space given to each partner.

3

KNOWING YOUR FINANCES

Before you can put together any financial plans for your future, you need to have a very clear picture of where you're starting from. This is what I mean by knowing your finances – understanding where your money is coming from, where it's going, and where it is when it's in your possession. It may sound like pretty basic stuff. But I'm somewhat horrified by the number of people who literally have no idea what's going on with their money! It's a classic example of burying your head in the sand and avoiding dealing with the important stuff.

Let's start with the important things to know:

- What money do you have coming in?
- What money do you have going out?
- What money have you saved?

If you've never done this before, it can feel a bit daunting, and there are plenty of reasons to put it off – not enough time, not enough know-how. But if you keep putting it off, you will never be able to take the next step in taking control of your finances. So, today is the day! I'll walk you through it.

You will need to get together:

- Bank Statements – for all accounts that have money coming in or out;
- Wage slips – if you have any employed earnings;
- Details of any online income that may not have got to your bank account yet – PayPal for example;
- Credit card and store card statements;
- Savings accounts – this can include premium bonds (I know I have premium bonds from when I was born!), any savings accounts including odd bits of money in a savings account from years ago, deposit accounts, Cash ISA's, investments;
- Pensions – now I know unless you are in your late 50s you can't get your hands on this cash just yet, but it's still worth fishing out a valuation. If you are employed, your wage slip should say how much your employer is paying in on your behalf as well.
- Supermarket vouchers - do you have any supermarket vouchers? I know I get a letter from Tesco's about once a quarter with something in it! Do you have a Christmas Saver Account with money in it? As Bruce Forsyth used to say: "What do points make? Prizes!" – well perhaps not prizes in this case, but they can be converted into things you need. We all love "buying" something with our Boots points!

So, once you have got everything together – it's pen and paper or spreadsheet time! I do like a good spreadsheet!

WHAT MONEY IS COMING IN?

Firstly document your income.

If you are self-employed or have your own limited company and pay yourself on an ad hoc basis, try and look at your income on a monthly basis. If that doesn't work for your situation, then calculate the amount in the way that best works for you then, if possible, break this down into a regular income.

If you have employed earnings, this information will be on your wage slip. Don't forget to include overtime if you receive it regularly.

You should come up with a total for your income, either per month or a time period that suits you.

WHAT MONEY IS GOING OUT?

A lot of people pay their bills on a monthly basis – usually this is because it best matches the way we receive our income. If you work on a different basis, then replace monthly with the frequency that you use.

Your outgoings will show on your bank statement and your credit card and store card statements, for those who have all three.

Use your bank statement first, as this will detail what we are going to class as "Essential" outgoings, such as your mortgage/rent, utility bills, petrol to get to work, insurances, food shopping etc.

If you aren't paying your "essential" bills monthly, can you get this changed? I know I used to pay my electricity bill quarterly and my water bill six monthly, but was paying myself monthly, so I contacted the providers and changed my payments to monthly to match. It made managing everything much easier.

From your bank and card statements, you should also be able to differentiate what we are going to class as "Lifestyle" outgoings, which are things like going out, clothes shopping, holidays and daily coffee from your local coffee shop.

Don't forget any standing orders you have set up to go into savings accounts, investments or your retirement planning strategy.

List your "Essential" and "Lifestyle" outgoings in two separate columns, so you can have a total for both.

Remember, what may be considered as an "Essential" outgoing for one person, may be a "Lifestyle" outgoing for another, these lists are personal to you.

Once you have all your outgoings listed, if you add them together, that will give you your monthly "Essential" and "Lifestyle" outgoings.

If you deduct the "Essential" figure from your Income total, it will hopefully give you the surplus cash you have left at the end of the month. This is what you are currently spending on "Lifestyle" outgoings, or perhaps saving.

Item	Essential	Lifestyle
Mortgage	£600	-
Pension	£80	-
Meals out	-	£80
Car payments	£150	-
Total	£830	£80
Overall total	£910	

If you add the total of the Essential and Lifestyle outgoings together, and deduct the total from your Income total, this will let you know what surplus you have, or not, with the lifestyle you are currently living.

The problem comes when your outgoings are higher than your income. Or when you would like to have more surplus cash left over than you have.

SAVINGS, PENSIONS AND INVESTMENTS

At the start of the chapter, we collated all your savings accounts, investments and pension information.

First things first, make sure that the statements show your correct details. Have you changed your name and not told them? Or most common of all, have you moved house and not told them?

There is £850 million of unclaimed money sitting in bank and building society accounts across the UK, and £19.4 billion in pension pots in the UK. Only 1 in 25 people instinctively think to tell their pensions providers about their new address. If you're sitting there thinking that this could be you, there are systems in place to help track down these funds. Check out our resources section on The Money Compass website for more details.

Make a list of the different accounts, and the amounts held in each, and if there is a purpose for the money in the account or investment vehicle, for example, university fees or retirement, then make a note of that as well.

We will come back to these later in the book.

CREDIT SCORE

Credit Score is a number which depicts a consumer's creditworthiness. The higher the score, the better you look to potential lenders.

They are statistically looking to see the probability of timely repayment of the loan. Your credit score can affect your ability to get a 0% interest rate credit card, and it will affect the rate you get for a mortgage.

Your credit score is calculated by taking into account your credit history, number of accounts you have open, the level of debt you have and your repayment history.

Do you know what your Credit Score is? When was the last time you checked it?

49% of the UK population have never checked their credit score (according to YouGov research conducted with 2,077 adults, February 2019). Doing so can help you understand your financial situation and give you a check against identity fraud.

There are only three agencies authorised in the UK to be able to check your Credit Score. These are Equifax, Experian and Transunion. There are companies such as ClearScore that will give you your credit score, but they use one of the three companies above to get this information for you. Your credit score is marked out of different amounts depending on which agency you use. As a rule of thumb, the higher your score the better. There are various apps and websites which will quickly and easily check your credit score for free.

Your credit score can be negatively affected if you have what is described as a "thin credit file". This means you haven't got any debt, or very little, and no credit card. When I ran my credit score recently, I noticed on my credit score report that since I closed my personal credit card and only use the joint one, which comes with my husband's credit card, I have no personal credit limit. This means that my credit score will decrease, which may cause problems with re-mortgaging or if I want to get a credit card or loan in the future.

Here are some top tips to help increase your credit score if you have a thin credit file:

- If you haven't already got a credit card, apply for one. If you can't get one, apply for a credit builder card. The interest rates will be higher, so make sure you pay it off each month. The purpose of a credit builder card, is to help build up a credit history. They usually have a low credit limit and a high APR (Annual Percentage Rate), so it's important to pay off the amount owed each month. Using it monthly, staying within the limit and paying the balance off each works positively towards your credit score.
- Spend a small amount on your credit card each month and pay it off each month. This shows the credit score agencies that you can reliably pay back money you borrow. Try and keep the amount you spend on your credit card under 30% of the amount you could borrow.
- Go through your Credit Score report and look for any mistakes and, if there are any, get these fixed.
- Electoral roll – if you're not already on the electoral roll, get yourself added – this makes you easier to verify and you appear more stable.
- If you get rejected for a credit card, don't apply for another straight away. When you apply, a mark is left on your credit report and lots of negative marks will have an impact on your Credit Score.
- Utility Bills – do you have any in your name? If not, then see if it's possible to put a couple of them in your name.

Keep an eye on your credit score, and review its progress.

BUSINESS FINANCES

We've looked at you knowing your personal finances, but it's also just as important to look at your business finances – maybe more so.

You should have separate bank accounts for your business. It makes life so much easier to keep your business accounts in order.

How you keep your business accounts used to be more flexible. However, with the introduction of Making Tax Digital you may find yourself needing to use accounting software. It's always best to check on the government website for the most up to date guidelines, or check with your accountant.

Whether you use accounting software or a good old spreadsheet – I think ledgers are a thing of the past now, although I do remember my mum completing one for my dad's business when I was younger – it's important to keep a track of your income and outgoings.

RECONCILING YOUR INCOME AND OUTGOINGS

Regularly reconciling your bank statement against your income and outgoings means you can keep a track of what's coming in and what's going out.

This is important for tracking income, especially if you don't get paid upfront. It will show you what money you have outstanding, so you can get chasing if necessary.

With your outgoings, I find it really helps to split these into "essential" and "workstyle" outgoings, much the same as when we were reviewing our personal finances. What are the essential costs which you need to run your business? Is there premises to pay for, professional indemnity insurance, a whole load of other insurances, regulatory costs, certification costs, equipment, stationery, marketing, tax, team members – whether you are outsourcing or employing? If you are employing, National Insurance contributions and pensions come in here too. Let's not forget health and safety!

This total gives you a number that you need to make each month to cover your essential expenses.

"Workstyle" expenses are those "nice to haves" which make your work life more pleasurable, but you could survive without.

Adding together your essential and workstyle outgoings, and deducting this from your income, will help you see if your business is making money or spending more than it's making.

If it is making money, then that's great! However, if it isn't, then the first step would be to go through the workstyle outgoings and see if you can trim anything, even if only on a temporary basis.

We will be covering the next steps in the Setting your Course chapter very shortly.

WHAT YOU KNOW NOW:

- What monies you have coming in, going out, and what savings and investments you have in place;
- The difference between Essential and Lifestyle outgoings;
- How to check your credit score, and what it means;
- How to reconcile your business finances.

4

YOUR FINANCIAL FOCUS

This is where the magic happens. This is where we make sense of everything we have talked about so far. What is your Financial Focus? What are you working towards? What do you want your life to look like?

For better or worse, almost all of our goals have a financial element to them, and this is where being financially savvy comes into its own.

What are your dreams and goals? These can be short terms goals or big, long-term goals, but we all have them. It's time for you to do some work again. Either grab a sheet of paper, or create yourself a vision board, and put on it EVERYTHING you want to achieve in life, every dream you have for what your life will look like.

Exotic holidays, a house with pillars and a wraparound veranda (ok, perhaps I've watched too many American films...), your dream car, a cleaner for your home, having a weekly flower subscription, private education for your children, pay off your mortgage early – the list is endless.

Take each aspect of your life and look at how you would like it to be. Let's say you already live in your dream home. Well, that is great, but there's bound to be another area of your life with some aspirations you're yet to fulfil. Think about: home, family time, holidays and travel, work life, retirement.

Home – are you in your dream home? What does your dream home look like? Can you picture it?

Family Time – do you have a big family that enjoy spending time together, holidaying together? Do long hours stop you spending as much time with your family as you wish?

Holidays and Travel – you may be a home bod and love time at home, or you may want to travel the world.

Work Life – are you working 80-hour weeks, burning yourself out and never having time off – is this the life you want to lead?

Retirement – possibly the biggest goal of all, do you know how you want this to look?

One of my big (actually, HUGE dreams) is to see all the different species of penguins in the wild. At the end of 2019, I had an amazing adventure to Antarctica, and when I got back, I felt very lucky to have seen eight different types of penguins – and to be honest, I thought that was it! I saw an emperor penguin, which I certainly didn't expect to see. Imagine, how I felt when I got home to find there are another nine different types of penguin to see in the world!!

So, after a bit of research, it looks like I need to visit the Galapagos Islands, the Sub-Antarctica Islands, New Zealand and South Africa to see each type of penguin in the wild.

That all sounds a bit daunting, but I have given myself a deadline of ten years, and I'm going to break it down into bite size goals. I'm not going to try and achieve all of those locations in one hit, but I feel it's much more realistic if I split it into three goals and three trips. The Galapagos Islands as one, South Africa another, and New Zealand and the Sub-Antarctica Islands as the third.

Look through your dreams. Can these be broken down into bite size goals? If you are currently renting and want a five-bedroom house with five acres, your first goal could be getting on the housing ladder, and from there, working up towards to that dream home.

Not all your dreams are going to be goals. I mean, if you dream of winning the lottery, there is an element of luck involved with this, although your odds of winning do improve if you buy a ticket – but is that really a goal? Let's focus on goals that you have some control over.

"A goal is a dream with a deadline"

PRIORITISING YOUR GOALS

By now, you should have a long list of dreams and goals. It's time to start prioritising them, or breaking them down into bite size goals.

Out of your goals, which ones are going to be goals you realistically want to achieve first? Let's also start putting together some deadlines for these goals.

Some deadlines may be simple to work out. You want to pay for private education for your two-year-old from when they reach the age of seven until they are 18 – you have a clear deadline of five years.

Other deadlines are more about you, for example, moving up the property ladder and moving from a two-bedroom house to a four-bedroom house as you start a family.

How about planning that six-week trip to Australia to visit family? Do you want to go next year or in three years' time?

Once you have added deadlines, it's time to do a reality check. Can you afford to fund your child's private education AND do a six-week trip to Australia? Do you need to move the deadline back on the trip to Australia? Or come up with a plan to close that financial gap.

RESEARCHING YOUR GOALS

Knowing your goals and your deadlines is a great start, but costing them out is the next stage of making these goals into a reality. How much is private education for a seven-year-old? Don't forget that it's likely that the cost today will have increased by the time the date to start arrives in five years' time - and this is a long-term investment, not just a one-off payment.

House prices change all the time; I know that the two-bedroom house I bought for £70,000 in 2001 was worth almost three times that 20 years later! Whilst none of us have a crystal ball, make sure the figure you are working towards takes potential increases into account.

When focusing on your goals, always make sure they are measurable, realistic and written down! Turn that vision board into a real list of prioritised goals, with dates, and keep that list safe.

WHAT YOU KNOW NOW:

- What a goal is (short term and a long term);
- How to prioritise your goals.

5

SETTING YOUR COURSE

So far, we have looked at the first three stages of working towards becoming financially savvy. Now it's time to pull it all together.

We've talked Money Mindset – understanding what your money mindset is, how to recognise your money blocks and how you can go about making changes so you can lead the life you want.

Next was Knowing your Finances, and we delved deep into all that paperwork to get a good understanding of where you are now financially, and what you already have in place for the future.

Then we looked at your Financial Focus; your dreams for the future, how to identify what can be turned into achievable goals, giving them deadlines, prioritising and researching the commitment needed to make them a reality.

Now it's time to Set your Course, and create a plan: what available money do you have to realise your goals? Do you need more? How can you achieve more?

If you don't have the available income to save the money you need to achieve your goals, one of two things needs to happen. You either need to have more income, or you need to cut your outgoings.

This time, we're going to start by looking at your business finances first before moving on to your personal finances.

BUSINESS INCOME

Whether you run a business with a team of staff, or you work alone, the same principles still apply.

After 20 years of running businesses, I have made plenty of mistakes. But out of the many companies that I have been involved with setting up, the majority of them are still running in some form or another, just not all with me still at the helm or even involved. All in all, I think I've got a pretty good track record as a business owner, and I'm happy to share my experience.

What happens when you have an idea for a business, you know that you will be good at doing whatever it may be, however the money side of it is a bit of a mystery? What should you charge for your services, for example? Often, we look around to find other people doing something similar and price somewhere around the same mark, then you open your doors (metaphorically) and you start trade.

Money starts coming in, you are over the moon, BUT you are working your ass off, and you don't ever seem to be taking any money home! Sound familiar?

The problem is that we've gone about it all wrong. Before we can calculate what we should be charging, we need to calculate what our business outgoings are going to be. Don't forget, you need to be making more than just the amount you want to live on. There's a list of other expenses which need paying before you do!

If you are nodding your head as you are reading this, then it's time to get things in order.

Once you have established your outgoings (refer back to the chapter Know your Finances for help), depending on what you do, you should be able to calculate a cost per client for the service or product you sell. For example, divide your total costs (including all your running costs) by the number of clients you can service a year, or products you think you can sell per month to give you a break-even number. But then, if you want a business worth running, you need to add a percentage to that figure to come up with the absolute minimum amount you *should* be charging.

This is an interesting exercise to carry out, particularly if you're already well into running your business and you're unsure of what the answers may be. Are you making or losing money at your current rates? Are you happy with your margin? Do you need to increase your prices? Coming back to Money Mindset, this can be a huge money block for some as we tend to undervalue the services we provide and end up in a circle of not achieving our full potential. Now is the time to change that!

BUSINESS OUTGOINGS

We've had a good look at business income, but your business outgoings need regular attention too. Are you paying for things you don't need? Did you sign up for a business membership that you just aren't using? Can you cancel it? Are you paying for networking which isn't working for you? Are you overpaying for your insurances – did you just let your renewal go through, without looking to see if you could save money by switching elsewhere?

Every month I complete a company outgoings spreadsheet where I go through each item and I make sure I know exactly what it is. I then assess each item and make sure the expenses are still relevant to the business.

A few years back our monthly outgoings reached a level that I really didn't feel comfortable with – our income had grown as well, but it was a real money block for me.

Up until that point, I had felt that if the worse happened, I would have the equivalent amount needed to pay the bills easily accessible. Then one month I was paying the team and the monthly invoices. The amounts involved had started getting higher and higher. Then one day the bank refused one of my payments, I had gone over the daily limit. All sorts of thoughts ran through my head: what if we don't have any income next month? What if all the team left, how would I manage all the work on my own?

Thinking objectively, I could see that these feelings were irrational and I couldn't come up with a logical scenario where our income would half, or even imagine the team all leaving. However, in my mind, it felt like I had moved from an amount I might find in the back pocket of my jeans (wouldn't that be nice!) to a figure which I wouldn't be able to find easily. It took me a good few weeks of telling myself that my thoughts were irrational before I could shake the feeling.

Nowadays, I pay out double that figure a month and don't bat an eyelid. I do wonder though, if I go through the next bank daily limit figure, will I have the same reaction, or will the mindset work I did back then see me through?

BUDGETING FOR BUSINESSES

Do you set yourself a budget for different areas of business? For example, do you agree an amount of money you want to spend on marketing for the year? It's good to plan ahead on what you want to spend, and what you want to spend it on. You can then factor that in to your cost calculations.

PAYING YOURSELF FIRST

If you haven't already read it, *Profit First,* by Michael Michalowicz, is a fascinating read. It looks at how to manage your business finances by taking your profit first, using a Cashflow Management system that you create for yourself. I'd highly recommend it.

Sometimes it helps to think about how you would treat yourself if you were an employee. If you were employed, you would be entitled to join an Auto Enrolment Pension Scheme, for example, and your employer would be paying at a minimum of 3% into the scheme for you, and you would be paying in 5%. As a business owner, don't you think that you deserve to treat yourself in the same way?

OTHER SOURCES OF INCOME

Apparently, the average entrepreneur has between five and seven different sources of income.

How many do you have? Is it possible to add more?

But what counts as a source of income? I wasn't sure, but when I thought about it, I was doing much better than I thought! I'm a service business, but my list is:

- One to one financial services clients;
- Digital solution – non advised;
- One to one estate planning clients;
- Digital guide to investing;
- Mentoring.

My second company (estate planning) was set up when I saw that our existing clients from our first company (financial advice) weren't getting the service they needed elsewhere, and we saw that we could not only ringfence our own clients but provide a much-needed professional service.

Look at your business. Is there something else that your existing clients could benefit from which you could provide?

When I set up The Money Compass, I could see there was a gap in the market. There was a whole group of women out there who weren't getting access to financial advice. I wanted to create a space which provided those women with the knowledge they needed to make financial decisions for themselves in a cost-effective way.

Is there such a gap in your market?

Another popular source of income is becoming an affiliate or an introducer for someone who offers a service that you don't, but would be of interest or benefit to your existing clients. If you go down this route, make sure you have a legal agreement in place to ensure that you not only get paid, but your clients receive the service you have said that they will get. It's your reputation on the line.

SETTING YOUR PERSONAL COURSE

We have looked at your business, now let's look at your personal finances.

PERSONAL INCOME

Alongside your business income, you may have income from other sources, such as property rental, maintenance payments and more. You will have established what these are when we looked at Knowing your Finances. It's important to take into account all of your sources of income when setting your course towards achieving your goals.

PERSONAL OUTGOINGS

In the Financial Focus section, you split your outgoings between "Essential" and "Lifestyle" outgoings.

Where can savings be made? Looking at your Lifestyle outgoings, how many of those can you stop?

It's time to be brutal. You have your goals planned out, you know how much they are going to cost you, and how much you need to save each month to achieve them.

The difference between your Income – Outgoings = the amount you have available to save, without doing any extra work on your income. If that amount isn't enough, you will need to go through your Lifestyle outgoings and see what you can do without.

Are you the person who likes to stop and buy a coffee each morning? How much is that coffee costing you? Could you make it at home instead before you left?

Do you buy your lunch out or from the supermarket each day? Is this something you could make at home?

With a daily coffee and lunch coming in at on average of £7.50 per day, if you did this five days a week for 48 weeks of the year, that comes to £1,800 per year!

In the next chapter we're going to look at some tips on how to create a monthly budget to help you look at your spending habits, and help you cut down those outgoings so you can start saving the money you want to achieve your goals!

WHAT YOU KNOW NOW:

- Potential ways to increase your sources of income;
- Calculating pricing;
- Why it's important to pay yourself first.

6

TIPS ON HOW TO CREATE A MONTHLY BUDGET

You now have a plan, so you know what you need to save. Let's look at some ideas to reduce the costs of your essential outgoings and look at ways to save money to keep those lifestyle outgoings down!

Really, a budget is the same as having a plan, but there can be lots of ways to help put that plan into action; some can sometimes be quite inventive.

ESSENTIAL OUTGOINGS

Mortgage

The biggest of your essential outgoings could well be your mortgage payments. When was the last time you reviewed your mortgage? Are you in a fixed rate mortgage, or has this ended and you are now paying a variable rate?

If you are not in a deal or a fixed rate mortgage, the best place to start is to get in touch with your current mortgage lender and see if they have any offers that would help save you some money on your mortgage. Alternatively, you could shop around or engage the help of an independent mortgage adviser to help you find the best deal for you.

Don't forget to review your life cover if you do make a change to your mortgage.

Utilities

Next up, your utility bills – when did you last review these? If you're not very good at remembering to do this, there are companies out there like Look After My Bills, who will do it for you. They review the market and recommend the best rate and provider for you at that time and, when that deal ends, they do it all over again!

Are your readings correct – is your electricity bill reading an estimate? When was the last time the meter was actually read? You may find you have a credit coming.

Many of us pay monthly for our utilities, and over the year the cost averages out – but do check if you are in credit and if so, by now much? That money can work harder for you somewhere other than sitting with the utility provider.

Insurance

We have lots of insurances in our life: life cover, house insurance, car insurance, pet insurance, you may have private medical insurance, and other insurances for white goods and boilers. These are usually renewed on an annual basis, and usually increase in cost – let's be honest, when was the last time any insurance renewal came in and it had gone down?

Don't just let the renewal date come and go and renew with the current provider without checking if it's still the best deal for you. There are many comparison sites out there. However, make sure you are comparing like for like, for example, if you have an existing excess of £100 for your car insurance, and the comparison site can save you a fortune, double check that the excess hasn't increased to £500!

If you find a better deal, but don't want the hassle of changing, contact your current provider first. You never know, they may match the new price for you so you don't have to change, but still benefit from the lower cost.

Council Tax

There's not usually much we can do about this one, but if you are living alone, are you getting the 25% discount? Is your property in the right band? Be careful with this one, our previous neighbours reported us to the council tax banding people as we had built an extension. The outcome was our band was increased from a D to an F – however they increased our neighbours too!

TV Licence

Just because you don't watch TV anymore, be careful as if you watch anything on BBC iPlayer you will still need a TV licence to watch it. Did you know, if you had a friend stay at your house and they plugged their laptop into your electrical socket and watched something on iPlayer, then you would have to have a TV licence? But if they just use their laptop battery then you're fine!!

LIFESTYLE OUTGOINGS

Online TV

I must be getting old, but it does seem like there are so many options out there – and you need to have an account with them all if you don't want to miss out on the latest cool series. But do you really need Sky, Netflix and Amazon Prime? If you're serious about saving, just pick one.

Online shopping

I covered this earlier in the book, but it definitely fits here as well. If you are prone to scrolling, spotting something you like, buying it immediately and then regretting the purchase when it arrives, try to delay hitting the pay button to the next day.

I have a bit of a Kickstarter addiction. For those of you who haven't come across Kickstarter before, it's a funding platform for creative projects. A project is created, and people can pledge money to make the project happen. There are usually "rewards" depending on the amount of money you pledge.

My addiction comes in fits and starts. Usually one item catches my attention, perhaps off the back of an email or when scrolling through Facebook, and then I'm on the website. For me it's like being a child in a sweetie shop. I make the purchases and then six months later goodies arrive in the post. I know, how many dresses, fleeces, t-shirts and shoes made from plastic bottles, coffee dregs, milk (!) and rags does one girl need?! I await in anticipation for my solar paneled video and camera enabled birdfeeder!

On a serious note, hide those ads on Facebook and delete those emails without opening them if you are going to be tempted by things you just don't need! I apologise in advance if you now feel the need to go and look up Kickstarter...

Amazon is my other big addiction. My husband is always complaining about our Amazon bill, but when I did a deep dive into what we were buying, it turned out it was mainly DVDs, boxsets and books. Well, there's nothing I can do about the books, but I could do something about the DVDs and boxsets... but this did mean dragging my husband into the 21st Century!

We already have Amazon Prime for the free delivery service, but we had never used it for their films and boxsets. I am slightly anal with our boxset watching, we usually have five different series on the go, and watch a disk from each and then rotate!

All I have done is replace the boxsets as we finish them with series that are free on Amazon. I also now include a recycled boxset. We have years' worth, and it seems silly to have them if we're not going to re-watch them.

We're doing exactly the same with our film watching. It's either free online or recycling the one's we already own. The Amazon bill has decreased dramatically!

Sale Items

I'm sure we can all relate to this one. You're out shopping and you end up in front of the sale rail eyeing up the items with a 50% discount. But are you really "saving" 50% if you didn't need the item in the first place? Or are you not saving anything but really spending that 50% figure when you don't need to?

I find that by walking away for a bit and reviewing in my head whether I actually need the item really helps to decide if I'm buying something I need, or something because it's in the sale.

Window Shopping

I don't like window shopping for big items if we're not actually going with the purpose of buying it; I just can't see the point in going. My husband is the opposite. He was test driving cars for four years before he bought his last car – he actually stopped a man in the car park at a National Trust property and ended up driving his car round the car park, to the raised eyebrows of me and the man's wife! He has no problem with popping into John Lewis to look at 75" televisions when we have no plans on buying one!

However, as much I dislike window shopping, I can see it's a good way of researching those big items that you have on your goal list and, a bit of win-win, it can be a good way of getting your shopping fix without actually spending the money. You can start planning and saving for that big item.

Subscriptions

Looking through your list of outgoings, how many subscriptions do you have? These can also be charitable donations. How many of those do you keep meaning to cancel but just don't ever seem to get round to it?

I subscribe to two magazines, both of which I read from cover to cover when they arrive.

However, I was paying £10 a month for a charity book subscription. When I joined it ticked two boxes, I was supporting a charity that I wanted to support AND I was getting a book every six weeks, and they did a discussion in a private Facebook group. After the first few books it was all going well, I read the books and was enjoying them and participated in the conversations. But then, I didn't enjoy one, nor the next, and my interest waned, but the £10 a month was still leaving my bank account.

Finally, the book *Life as a Unicorn* appeared in the post, and it was the push I needed. Now, before I get stoned for criticising *Life as a Unicorn*, I have to confess I haven't read it yet! It's still on the "to be read" pile and it may be a great book, but it was the straw that broke the camel's back. I logged into my bank account and cancelled my regular payment there and then!

Membership subscriptions are also one to watch, but remember to check the small print; you may have signed up for a set period of time. If you have, make a diary note on your phone to cancel when that period has ended.

If you do find yourself in that situation, see if you can get the most from the membership whilst you are a member. You never know, you might re-discover what made you join in the first place.

App subscriptions on your phone

How many times have you seen a transaction appear on your bank statement or your credit card for an amount you don't recognise and it turns out to be for an app that you aren't using anymore, but haven't cancelled?

I can certainly raise my hand at this one, and isn't it annoying! Now I check about once a month what apps I am subscribed to on my phone, and unsubscribe from anything I'm not using. Remember to watch out for those 7-day and 30-day free trials as well; those periods of time always seem to fly by far too quickly!

Food Shopping budget tips

Online food shopping is more popular at the moment, and this is a great budgeting method. Rather than just wandering around the shop picking up items and putting them in your trolley, only finding out the total when you get to the till, you are much more in control. A good plan is to set yourself a weekly budget, and don't go over it.

Alternatives for getting the retail buzz

I'm an avid reader and love books – in fact, if I'm not feeling 100% and feel like I need a bit of retail and fancy a shopping spree the most likely place I will end up is in a book shop!

The other year I found a great alternative, which not only saved me money but also hit the spot!

Car boots! We have a large car boot near where I live. There is a great book stall that sells books for £1 or £2 and they always seem to have my favourite authors and types of books! But the best bit is finding someone who doesn't come very often selling books 50p, or 3 for £1. I can spend a fiver and come home with 10 books! It's all very satisfying.

Loyalty cards

When I think about loyalty cards the one that always pops to mind for me is the Boots card. For every £1 you spend on a "qualifying product" you get 4 points – some items you only get 1 point per £1. Each point is worth a penny when you go to spend them in store.

I used to save up my Boots points to use at Christmas time, when they had all the "buy 2 get one free" offers. Saved me a fortune each year.

A lot of supermarkets have loyalty cards which can now be used not just in store, but on all sorts, including holidays. I have friends who go canal boating every year with their Tesco Clubcard points!

Credit Cards with benefits

Lots of credit cards nowadays come with point systems. I have a Virgin Atlantic credit card for the miles, which means I usually fly to America once a year premium economy for free (I just have to pay the tax). Tesco's credit card gives you Clubcard points for every £8 you spend on the credit card (more if in Tesco).

Cashback Apps

Cashback Apps are apps which allow you to get a percentage of your money back when spending at certain stores and on certain websites.

There is a wide range of Cashback Apps available out there, like TopCashBack, where you either shop through the app, or you can link your card to the app, and when you shop in certain shops you receive cashback. At time of writing Tesco have a special offer with TopCashBack where on a purchase of £15 or more, you get 8% cashback.

I've covered lots of ways of cutting existing expenses and looking at how you could change some of your spending habits, but can your spending in the past be used to recoup some monies back now?

Each year, I have a spring clean, and I don't mean with a duster and a hoover - I have a cleaner for that! I'm talking about my belongings. I go through my clothes and make decisions on what I will never wear again. Things I think I would wear but can't fit into, go into boxes then it's like having a new wardrobe when my weight changes and I go through the boxes!

However, my husband is a total hoarder - especially when it comes to clothes, so I now do a neat trick. As already mentioned, I am quite anal and all our clothes hangers face the same way (of course they do), so I turn all the hangers to face the opposite way, and once the item of clothing has been worn, washed and returned to the wardrobe, I hang it the way it should be hanging. That way, after a year, I can see which clothes haven't been worn.

This works well in two ways, I don't just wear the same shirt/t-shirt all the time, but I also then know what isn't being worn, and it can go.

Selling your clothes and other items can be done through many different websites, eBay, probably being the most popular. The other alternative is a car boot which can make for a fun morning out.

For books, DVDs and CDs there is also apps like Ziffit and Music Magpie, who agree a set price for the item when you scan the barcode. You then just box up the items and drop them off at a collection point, and they pay you money once they have received them.

This list is certainly not exhaustive, but I hope will give you some food for thought with ways that you can save or even make some extra money.

WHAT YOU KNOW NOW:

- How to make savings with your essential outgoings;
- How to make savings with your lifestyle outgoings;
- How to make money while saving.

7

DEBT VS. SAVINGS

Debt vs. savings is an age-old debate and, as with everything financial, there isn't a straight-forward answer; there are a lot of elements to consider.

Let's start with looking at the biggest debt that most of us will have: your mortgage.

When my husband was younger and bought his first house, his primary focus was to save enough money to pay off the mortgage. He saved and saved until he had enough money. He had achieved his goal, but then he didn't pay off his mortgage! Once he knew he could do it, he didn't feel the need to do it!

However, many people have a money block about paying their mortgage off, and it becomes the most important thing they need to do. My parents wanted to clear their mortgage as soon as possible and reduced their 25-year mortgage to a 15-year term mortgage by overpaying.

So, what's wrong with wanting to clear your mortgage as soon as possible? Well, nothing. But there are a few things to consider first.

Firstly, don't forget to check if you have an early repayment charge – you don't want to be paying an unexpected fee. An early repayment charge is a penalty that may be applied to your mortgage if you decide to pay off or overpay your mortgage above an agreed amount. It usually applies when you are tied into a special rate, like a fixed rate.

What is your mortgage rate? You can do a very quick search online to see what the average mortgage rate currently is, to see whether you have a low or a high mortgage rate.

If you have such a low interest rate, could those mortgage overpayments be working harder elsewhere?

Let's look at an example of John and Janet – remember those Ladybird books when you were growing up?

John and Janet have a mortgage of £100,000 with a mortgage rate of 1.5%. They have a credit card balance of £5,000 with an APR of 20% of which they are paying the minimum premium each month. They want to overpay their mortgage each month by £200.

In the above circumstances the best thing to do would be to use the £200 per month to pay off the credit card rather than the mortgage. The interest rate on the credit card is far higher than the mortgage, and will be growing against the debt each month.

Let's use a different example, with John and Janet again:

John and Janet have a mortgage of £100,000 with a mortgage rate of 1.5%. They have no credit card debt. They have £200 each month spare. John wants to use it to overpay the mortgage, and Janet has found a savings account that will pay an interest rate of 3.5% and she wants to save it into that instead.

In this example, Janet is right. The £200 per month will be working harder for them in the savings account than by using it to overpay the mortgage. Plus, the added win, if they need a quick injection of cash they have instant access to the money, whereas once it's been used to overpay the mortgage, they can't get it back.

Another option if you are really focused on paying off your mortgage payments, is an offset mortgage. An offset mortgage is where you have a mortgage and a savings account with the same lender. The money in the savings account is used to reduce the amount of mortgage interest charged.

These work really well as they still give you access to the money you are overpaying, as it's going into a savings account running alongside your mortgage. It doesn't earn any interest, however; from an interest point of view, the lender treats the money you pay into the account as if it has been paid off the mortgage. There is no interest payable on the savings account.

GOOD DEBTS AND BAD DEBTS

Who knew that some debts are "good" debts? Debts such as mortgages are classed as just that. Student loans are another debt that is considered a "good" debt. You don't start paying your student loan until you are earning over the threshold amount.

Let's concentrate on those "bad" debts now.

The rule of thumb is to clear your "bad" debts first.

"Bad debts" are debts such as credit cards, store cards and overdrafts. These usually have high interest rates, meaning the debt can grow quickly. That's why it's best to get these clear first.

If you are paying a high level of interest on a credit card, the first step is to see if you can do a balance transfer to a 0% interest rate credit card. This is usually for a set period of time, before the rate will increase to a higher level. By doing this, at least your debt will not be growing while you pay it off.

If you can't get a 0% interest rate credit card, see if it's possible to get one with a lower interest rate than the one you currently have.

If your situation is looking dire and you can't see an end in sight, communication is key. Speak to the credit card companies, speak to the bank, see if you can come to an arrangement.

If they aren't willing to listen, there are organisations that can help such as StepChange.

Where does bad debt come from?

Having an action plan in place to clear your debts is all well and good, but you need to look into how the debt came about in the first place.

I have clients who have paid off all their "bad" debt during the pandemic because they haven't been able to go out and spend their money on days out, holidays and all the other things they used to spend their money on. Not only have their cleared their debt, but have more in savings than ever before. Moving forward, they are conscious of the habits they had, and the new one's they have created, and plan not to get back into debt as they go out and about more.

Certainly in 2020 and 2021, the world has been a difficult place, and your debt may be due to circumstances outside your control. A reduced income may have forced you to spend on credit cards.

However, if that's not the case, then it's time to have a good hard look at your spending habits. This goes back to the work we talked about right at the start of the book when we talked about Money Mindset.

Does money burn a hole in your pocket? Is your credit card an extension of your wallet? Does window shopping always end in a purchase? Do sales excite you?

Paying off your debt only to then create it again will just create a vicious circle and will never end well. You need to break that circle.

In the Tips for Monthly Budgeting chapter, we looked at ways to manage online shopping. Perhaps give your credit card to a responsible friend or family member to hold on to for you in case you have an emergency?

Try setting yourself a budget for personal spending and stick to it. Many bank accounts have pots now; move the amount you have set aside for spending each month into a separate account, and only take that card out with you when you're shopping.

WHAT YOU KNOW NOW:

- The difference between good and bad debt;
- How to look objectively at your debt situation and make the right decision.

8

EMERGENCY FUNDS AND JAR SAVING

WHAT IS AN EMERGENCY FUND?

I'm sure that you've all heard of having an emergency fund, but what is one, how much should you have in it, and where should you keep it?

An emergency fund is your safety net for when there is just that -an emergency. This could be being unable to work, your car breaking down and needing repairs, or the boiler breaking; it could be anything!

It's recommended that you have three months' worth of your regular essential outgoings in your emergency fund. However, an emergency fund is individual to you and it's important to work out the right figure for your circumstances.

Because you are most likely to need this money in an emergency, it's important to have easy access to some, if not all, of it rather than having it tied up in a notice account. Good options for this would be an easy access or instant bank or building society account, or premium bonds are also a good option.

A word of warning though, make sure you don't end up with too much money in your emergency fund, with it sitting in an instant access account. At current interest rates, it will be making little or no interest; you want to make sure your money is working as hard as it can for you.

JAR SAVINGS

Did you have a piggy bank when you were little? I had a cream ceramic one with pink roses on it and I used to save 10p coins in it! Well, I'm a big believer that the concept of a piggy bank is just as apt for adults.

I bought my husband one of those big jars which you can have personalised that you have to break to get into it. It's got "Ralph's Las Vegas Fund" on it. It replaces a smaller one he had before which he filled with £2 coins. However, it is getting harder to fill as we are using less and less physical money.

The modern-day equivalent would be a bank account where you can label different "pots" and "jars" and put money away each month to save for the different goals that you have. These are becoming more and more common. Set up a standing order for the day after you pay yourself to make sure the money is put away in the right "pot" before you look to see what you have to spend during the month. It's a case of out of sight, out of mind; if you leave it in your account until the end of the month it is likely to get spent.

WHAT YOU KNOW NOW:

- What an emergency fund is and why it's important;
- How much to have in your emergency fund;
- How to jar save.

9

THE BANK OF MUM AND DAD
(AND OTHER THINGS NOT TO RELY ON OR DO!)

We have established your financial goals, and you have a plan in place to achieve those, but here I want to look at some things that people have done in the past thinking they were a good idea to help them achieve those goals.

THE BANK OF MUM AND DAD

Unfortunately, over the years that I have worked in financial services I have come across this far too many times.

"I'll pay my mortgage off when my parents die."

"My parents will bail me out, they always have in the past."

"I don't need to worry about my retirement plans, my parents will be dead by then and I'll get the house and all their money."

It makes me feel incredibly sad when I hear quotes like these.

Whilst the Bank of Mum and Dad will have served many of us over the years, and I'm no exception – my dad was guarantor on my first mortgage when I was 18 – it can become a real problem when misused/misunderstood/relied upon in the wrong way.

When I moved house and re-mortgaged in 2001, I realised that I earnt more money than my parents did. When I took mum out, I used to treat her rather than expecting her to treat me.

However, my story aside, if your parents are wealthy, why shouldn't you rely on the Bank of Mum and Dad?

A few years ago, we had an elderly couple as clients. The wife was 15 years younger than the husband, and it was the third marriage for the husband. The assumption by all the family was that the husband would be the first to die, as he was that much older than his wife. His will left everything to his wife or, in the event of her dying first, then everything went to his two children.

The assumption by the two children was that the wife, their step-mother, had an identical will.

However, as it happened, the wife sadly died first. We went to see the husband and the children after the wife had died, and it was certainly an interesting meeting. The wife's will had been read, only for the children to discover that, like her husband's will, she had left everything to him. However, in the event of him prede-ceasing her, she had left everything to charity. The children would have received nothing. The estate size was approximately £2,000,000.

The two children had already been spending their inheritance before their father died a year later. I wouldn't wish death on anyone, however, am I alone to secretly wish he had gone first?!

Where there are families with children from first and second marriages, getting the correct wording in the will is so important; the expectation of receiving anything may be misplaced.

OLD AGE CARE

Today people are living longer but they are, unfortunately, not always healthier. The number of people having to move into a care home or needing live in carers is on the increase, and the cost of care isn't cheap. The average cost of a residential care home comes in at over £2,800 per month, and nursing care homes even higher. Live-in carers come in even higher still.

When you write down your life goals and what you want to achieve in retirement, not many of us write down going into a care home, and your parents will be no different. That inheritance that you are relying on from the Bank of Mum and Dad as part of your long-term strategy, may all be eaten up before it even gets to you!

LOTTERY WIN

We all like the idea of winning the lottery. I remember a roll over week a few years back with a total of £93 million! Wow, what I could do with that! I remember thinking about it all week, mentally noting all the friends and family members that I would be able to help, the charities I would support, and of course the difference it would make in my own life. But Friday night came and went, and someone else was £93 million richer. I just hope that they were as altruistic as I was planning to be!

Much as I enjoyed the planning and the dream, winning the lottery isn't a great plan for the future. First things first, you need to buy a lottery ticket to be in with a chance of winning it! Second there is a 1 in 45 million chance of winning the big one! Unfortunately, a lottery win should not part of your financial plan for the future!

WHAT YOU NOW KNOW:

- Why you shouldn't rely on the Bank of Mum and Dad;
- The importance of realistic goals.

WHEN TO INVEST, AND WHEN TO SAVE

INVESTING AND SAVING – WHAT'S THE DIFFERENCE?

Rule of thumb (and let's be honest, who doesn't like a good rule of thumb?), savings are usually for short-term goals, such as an emergency fund, or for a goal which you want to achieve in five years or less.

You shouldn't be looking to invest unless you are prepared to not touch the money for five years or more – investing is a much longer-term approach.

SAVINGS FOR SHORT TERM GOALS

We covered how much to have saved for an emergency fund in an earlier chapter, but there are many other short-term goals that you may have. For example, saving for a deposit for a house, buying a new car or a holiday.

All of these are goals which you will usually be looking to achieve within five years.

You may be wondering why you need to invest if you have savings. If you're achieving your short-term goals that way, surely, it's a good approach for your long-term goals, like your retirement, too?

The main reason we look at savings for short-term goals, but not long-term goals, is inflation risk. We will come on to risk in a later chapter, but when looking at savings, it's really important to touch on this here.

WHAT IS INFLATION?

The easiest way to describe inflation is as a rise in the overall level of prices for the goods and services consumed by a household. It is caused by demand exceeding supply, increase in prices, or if the government is in debt and printing more of its own money.

When inflation is low, interest rates on savings accounts will be low, however it also means that mortgage interest rates will be lower. When inflation is high, interest rates on savings accounts will increase, however, so will mortgage rates.

You can see next how, over time, inflation impacts on the things that you buy.

May 1989	Food prices comparison	May 2019
49p	Loaf of white bread	£1.09
£1.89	Chicken (per kg)	£2.77
28p	Milk (per pint)	44p
17p	Oranges (each)	38p
£1.06	Pint of lager	£3.69

When you are saving it's very difficult to beat inflation, which means that the "buying power" of your money is decreasing as time goes by.

The graph below compares the Bank of England base rate against the Consumer Price Index (in effect, inflation). As you can see, the cost of inflation is higher than the value of your savings.

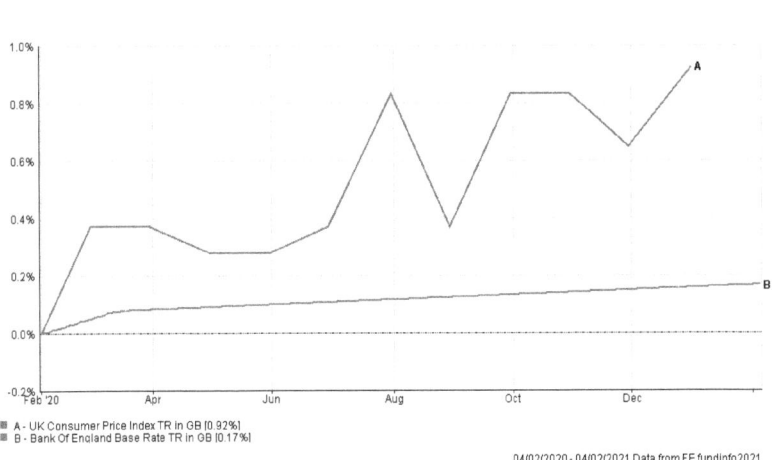

Pricing Spread: Bid-Bid • Data Frequency: Daily • Currency: Pounds Sterling

■ A - UK Consumer Price Index TR in GB [0.92%]
■ B - Bank Of England Base Rate TR in GB [0.17%]

04/02/2020 - 04/02/2021 Data from FE fundinfo 2021

SHORT TERM SAVINGS OPTIONS

One of my favourite options for short term savings is Premium Bonds. I grew up hearing about ERNIE, the Premium Bond machine which would spit out the winning numbers each month. I still have my Premium Bonds from when I was born, and I remember having money from my 18th birthday and not knowing what to do with it – I saved £100 into Premium Bonds!

Premium Bonds can only be bought from National Savings and Investments (NS&I) they are essentially a government run lottery bond. The government pays 1% per annum interest, and this is the amount of money which is used as tax free winnings on a monthly basis.

Currently the odds of winning are 34,500 to 1 (for every £1 bond). The prizes range from £25 to £1 million! Since December 2020 there has been a lot of speculation on whether it's worth it. Personally, with interest rates as low as they are, I'm happy to have a punt!

INDIVIDUAL SAVINGS ACCOUNTS (ISAS)

Everyone over the age of 16 can have a Cash ISA, and has an annual allowance – which is the maximum that can be paid into any ISA for that tax year.

The main benefits of a Cash ISA are that they are tax free, they usually come with instant access and usually have a higher interest rate compared to other instant access savings accounts.

LIFETIME ISAS

Lifetime ISAs were introduced in April 2017. I remember this as, when they were first announced, I was considering signing up for one, only to realise that I had passed 40 in the February and was therefore too old to have one! They are only available to those aged between 18 and 40, and you have an annual allowance, which is part of your overall ISA allowance.

The way they work is that you can pay in up to the Lifetime ISA annual allowance per annum, and the government will add 25% to the amount (subject to the maximum per year), up until you are 50. You can use the money to buy your first house, or to save for later life. If you wish to take the money out for any other reason there is a 25% penalty.

OTHER SAVINGS ACCOUNTS

There are a huge range of savings accounts out there, some with instant access, others which have notice periods and others fixed periods. The accounts with longer notice periods or longer fixed rates will pay out the higher levels of interest, but beware, if you need access earlier it may well be at the cost of any interest earned. So before signing up for a savings account with a longer notice period or fixed period, make sure you know what you are signing up for and what the penalties are.

Emergency funds should always be instant access.

TAX ON SAVINGS ACCOUNTS

There are personal savings allowances on interest and tax payable on savings accounts. This means there is an amount you can save before you begin to be charged tax on the interest earned on your savings accounts. These allowances change annually so it's always best to check on the government website for the most up to date information.

As you can see, there is a variety of options open to you when looking at short-term saving options. Don't forget to do your research and pick the options that best suit your circumstances.

WHAT YOU KNOW NOW:

- When to save and when to invest;
- What inflation is;
- What different short-term savings options are available to you.

11

INVESTING: THE THREE WAYS TO MAKE MONEY

When you look to invest, there are three major things to consider: Time, money and risk.

TIME - "The stock market is a device for transferring money from the impatient to the patient."

Warren Buffett

MONEY - "Money makes money. And the money that makes money makes more money."

Benjamin Franklin

RISK - "Successful investing is about managing risk, not avoiding it." Benjamin Graham

TIME

When you look back at your financial focus and what your long-term goals are, how much time have you given yourself?

The more time you can have, the more likely you are to achieve those goals.

I have a team that work with me and for the past ten years, we have had a pension scheme available for them all. When the government launched Auto Enrolment pension schemes, the minimum age to be eligible to join was 22. However, companies could let younger staff join. I always encourage even my youngest staff, at 18 and 19, to join the pension scheme as soon as possible. They are giving themselves the best possible start for planning for their future.

One of my team, doesn't just pay in the 4% (plus 1% tax relief from the government), she doubled her contributions in and at 28, has a pension projection at retirement of £300,000, not taking into account any increases.

By having time on your side, you can benefit from what Albert Einstein allegedly called the "eighth wonder of the world" – compound interest.

WHAT IS COMPOUND INTEREST?

Compound interest is the interest earned on interest previously earned that you have left invested.

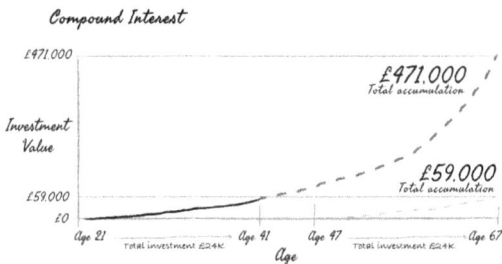

The graph above demonstrates why starting early is really important. The two examples above both invested the same amount of money over the same period of time, however the person who invested when they were younger was able to benefit for a longer period of time accumulating wealth purely from the compounded interest.

As each year passes, the interest (or growth) is kept within the investment, and the following year, the interest is added to the figure from the previous year, so interest is then paid on a greater overall amount. This continues all the time your money is invested until you need money from that investment.

In short, the longer the investment can grow, the better – it's also known as the snowball effect.

CALCULATING COMPOUND INTEREST

Normally, I would be saying get a spreadsheet, but there is a relatively simple way to work out how long it will take to double your money if you invest a certain amount and you know what return you will be getting. It's called the Rule of 72.

Take the number 72, divide it by the expected percentage return, and this will give you the number of years it will take you to double your money.

Say you have an amount to invest, and you are expecting a return of 6% per annum, to calculate how long it will take to double your money, you would do the following calculation:

$72 / 6 = 12$

This means that it will take 12 years to double your money.

It can also be used the other way round. Say you are offered something that sounds a bit too good to be true – unfortunately it usually means that it is! But with the Rule of 72 you can check it out by doing the calculation in reverse.

For example, you are told that someone can double your money in three years. Take 72 and divide by the number of years, in this case 3 years – 72/3 = 24%. They are offering a 24% return, and let's be honest, that does sound a bit too good to be true!

Another quote allegedly from Einstein about compound interest is: "He who understands it, earns it; he who doesn't, pays it."

Now, don't panic, if you are reading this and you haven't started thinking about your future, and are the other side of 40 or even 50: there is still time. But other factors will need to play a role in getting you there.

MONEY

The second way to make money is...money! Having money in the first place is always going to make it easier to get more. Compound interest is an excellent example of how that works!

However, having money isn't always the problem; it's what you do with it when you have it. Earlier in this book we have covered money mindset, knowing your finances, getting your financial focus and setting your course. By following these really important steps, you should have the money to invest in your future.

Now, I know that the money mindset "you have to work hard to make money" is scoffed at by many, however I do believe that working hard doesn't have to mean burying yourself in work so you can't cope. I believe you can work hard at being savvy with your business decisions and your financial future.

There are many business mentors out there who talk about how to make money, and how to create a passive or semi-passive income business. However, when you listen to what they have to say, it still involves an element of hard work to get everything in place. It doesn't just happen overnight by magic.

If you have money, it's important to make sure it's working as hard for you as possible. I have had clients who have come to me in the past with over £200,000 sitting in their current account.

As I write this, the current interest rate in the UK is 0.1%. This is one of the lowest levels since the interest base rate was started in 1694. Compare this with an inflation rate of 2.4%, this money could have been working a lot harder for that client over the years.

RISK

The third way to make money when looking at investing is to consider and increase the level of risk which you are taking with your money.

Why is risk important? Well, as a rule of thumb, over a long period of time the more risk you are willing to take, the higher the returns will be.

Risk is very personal to you and what is right for one person may not be right for another – stories of "my friend said she does this, and I should do the same", always bring me out in a cold sweat – your friend's circumstances and views towards risk may well be completely different from yours, and following blindly is not the best thing to do.

The best starting place is to complete an investment risk questionnaire – see the resources section on the Money Compass website for some options with this.

Once you have completed the investment risk questionnaire, it will give you an outcome describing your level of risk and outlining an asset allocation that someone with that risk profile would be comfortable with. However, it's important to note that if you don't feel that outcome describes you, and in fact, it makes you feel a bit sick and scared, then the questionnaire results do not define you. It is just a starting point – read the descriptions below and above your outcome and see if you feel more comfortable with those instead.

Eventually, you should have a risk outcome which you feel comfortable with.

Essentially, the higher the number which the questionnaire comes out with, the more risk you feel comfortable with taking. But risk isn't the only consideration when calculating your attitude towards investment risk. The other area which works hand in hand with investment risk is your capacity for loss.

WHAT IS CAPACITY FOR LOSS?

Capacity for Loss is how you would feel if you invested, say, £50,000, and a year later your annual statement arrived in the post, and it had dropped in value. Say it had dropped to £45,000, so a 10% decrease, how would this make you feel?

How would you feel if it had dropped to £30,000 – 40%?

Now, some of you may be horrified by both of these drops, but some of you may be thinking: *well, it's invested in the stock market which goes up and down, I don't want the money at the moment, I invested for the long term, and historically the market goes up.*

Different risk levels come with different potential amounts of loss, and it's important to not only be comfortable with the risk description for you, but also how you would feel if your investment dropped in value by an amount.

The below graph shows what the potential losses could be against each of the risk outcomes.

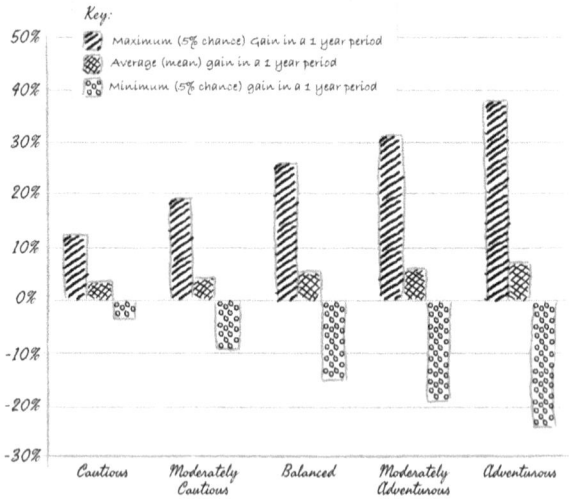

In March 2020, the UK stock market fell by more than 10% in a single day - that's the most it had fallen in one day since 1987 (technically a stock market crash is more than 10% in one day). Overall, in March it dropped by over 34% but, important to remember here, by the end of March, it had bounced back again.

The natural thing that people want to do is to get their money out and bury it under their mattresses, but this is the worst thing that you can ever do. Imagine taking your money out after it had lost 34% only for rates to bounce back three weeks later – how are you going to get that 34% back now?

If you re-invest, then you will be investing at the higher price, so that potential for growth has gone.

If you can hold your nerve, and have the appetite for it, then following the words of one of my personal heroes, Warren Buffett, is a good thing to do. But **only** if you have the attitude to do so.

'Be fearful when others are greedy, and be greedy when others are fearful.'

I've talked about what your investment attitude to risk is and the importance of making sure you feel comfortable with the level of risk you are looking to take. However, there are times when you may want to look at taking a slightly higher level of risk.

The first of these would be if you are young and have a lot of years until you will want to touch your investment, for example if the money is being invested for your retirement. Investing in a higher risk now would see your investment going up and down more, but historically, over the long term, research has shown that investments do rise, and as a rule, more risk = more reward!

The other time, is when you don't have time on your side and the amount of money you have is limited.

Risk could be the answer – but remember it can't work miracles!

From the graph on the previous page showing capacity for loss, it also shows capacity for growth. The higher the level of risk you are prepared to take, the more growth you potentially could have with your investment.

You will have a figure that you are working to achieve, and the lower levels of risk may not be able to get you to that figure. By raising the level of risk you are prepared to take, and the amount you are prepared to lose, you may be able to get to that amount.

DIFFERENT LEVELS OF INVESTMENT RISK

Your feelings about the risk you are willing to take might be different depending on what pot of money we are talking about – you may be willing to take a higher level of risk with your pension, as you know you can't access it for, say, 15+ years.

However, you may feel a bit more cautious about the level of risk you would be willing to take on your savings account, knowing that if you lost a lot of money, you may not be able to go on that holiday of a lifetime when you reach a milestone birthday in a few years!

WHAT YOU KNOW NOW:

- The three ways to make money – Time, Money and Risk;
- What compound interest is;
- Understanding capacity for loss and different levels of risk.

12

INVESTMENT ASSET ALLOCATION

Following on from investment risk, and looking at what is the right level of risk for you, the next natural step is looking at what to invest in. And the first part of that puzzle is knowing how to match your level of risk with the different options available.

There are many investments out there that offer a portfolio to match your risk and do all the work for you, but I believe that understanding the mechanics behind that is really important.

So, let's look at Investment Asset Allocation.

First things first, what is an asset?

An asset is something that investors can buy and sell. Assets are split into asset classes; this is a group of assets that are similar and subject to the same laws and regulations.

WHAT IS INVESTMENT ASSET ALLOCATION?

Asset Allocation is an investment technique that balances risk versus reward by adjusting the percentage of each asset in an investment portfolio according to the investor's risk and investment goals.

Having different percentages in different assets helps with diversification - or in plain English, it's about not putting all your eggs in one basket!

Don't panic if that sounds all a bit terrifying, there are lots of options out there that do the hard work for you. Let's talk about what the different assets are – in the industry, we call these asset classes. Think of it like different subjects at school.

There are many different asset classes, however, to keep things nice and simple, I'm going to split them into six main ones:

- Cash
- Fixed Interest
- Property
- UK Equities
- Developed Markets
- Emerging Markets

Each of these six asset classes has a different level of risk, starting with Cash as the lowest risk, and Emerging Markets (which is investing in countries such as Brazil, Russia, India and China) as the highest risk.

CASH

Cash is the only asset class which doesn't have the risk of dropping in value, however cash is not risk free. It can be affected by inflation, meaning the amount of cash you have will not go down, but the buying power of that cash can go down.

At the time of writing, interest rates are at an all-time low, and there's even talk of negative interest rates. This is definitely a risk that can't be ignored.

The other risk when investing in cash is the risk of the company the money is held with defaulting. Remember 2008 and Northern Rock? Watching the news with queues of customers queuing outside to withdraw their savings? The government bailed out Northern Rock, but it was an important lesson to many that banks weren't as invincible as many thought.

The good news is that there is some protection against losing all your investment should a bank fail. The Financial Services Compensation Scheme will compensate up to £85,000 per eligible person, per bank.

FIXED INTEREST

When I say Fixed Interest, I don't mean like a bank account paying a fixed interest rate, but things like corporate bonds and government bonds, and not just the UK.

Corporate bonds are when an investor loans a company money for a fixed period and will receive a defined return. For example, a Tesco 10-year bond paying 5.5%. The bond would run for 10 years and the investor would receive 5.5% per year for the 10 years, and then get their money back. These are usually bought by funds in bulk, rather than by individuals.

Cash and Fixed Interest are considered lower risk investments, both offering potentially lower returns over the long term. However, they are good as income providers and protecting against the volatility of higher risk elements.

PROPERTY

Property is always an interesting one. Its biggest risk is illiquidity risk (which means that it can be difficult to get your money back from it if you need it in a hurry), especially for those funds which are invested in actual bricks and mortar properties. A lot of the large funds are invested in property such as shopping malls and huge office blocks, as well as mix of smaller properties. This caused problems back in 2008 and again in 2020, where the property funds were suspended, and people were unable to get their money out of these funds.

Property is best for a long-term investment and not suitable for short term investments.

EQUITIES

This is when you invest in shares within companies, such as FTSE 100 companies and further afield. The level of risk within the types of equities available is extremely varied.

I have split this into three areas:

UK EQUITIES

UK Equities are invested in UK based companies. These can be FTSE 100 companies, or smaller companies who have shares. Broadly speaking, the bigger the company, the lower the risk, however this can all change depending on what is happening in the economy!

DEVELOPED MARKETS

Developed Market equities are invested in shares in companies based in countries such as France, Germany and North America.

My husband described this best as "countries where you would be happy to drink water from the tap".

Companies that they could be invested in include Apple, BMW, Facebook, Coca Cola – again this could be a mixture of large and smaller companies.

EMERGING MARKETS

Finally, the highest risk asset class I have mentioned, Emerging Markets. This is when the fund invests in shares in companies in countries such as Brazil, Russia, India and China.

Or, as my husband would say, countries where you wouldn't drink from the tap, and buying bottled water would be the way forward!

An emerging market economy is one that is moving from a low income, less developed economy to a modern, higher standard of living one.

Getting your asset allocation right is one of the most important parts of creating a portfolio, and in some respects, is more important than picking the funds which are placed under each asset class – which is where diversification comes into play.

Usually (though not when there is a global pandemic), when one asset class goes down, another will go up to cushion the movement in the market.

Asset Allocation goes hand in hand with your attitude to investment risk when building a portfolio of funds to invest in. For example, if you are a low-risk investor, you would have fewer or even no emerging markets funds in your portfolio.

Knowing the makeup of your portfolio is important if you want to avoid any surprises. I had a client come to me. We ran the Investment to Risk questionnaire, went through Capacity for Loss, and had a discussion, and they came out very low risk.

They told us they didn't like to take too much risk, and hadn't done so in the past. We carried out a full analysis of their investments and imagine our surprise to discover that the majority of their money was invested in Asia! It was all in emerging markets, with no diversification, making it a very high-risk portfolio for someone with a high-risk attitude to investment risk, let alone someone with a very low attitude to investment risk!

If you haven't already completed your investment risk questionnaire on The Money Compass website, then please feel free to do so, the outcome will also give you an asset allocation breakdown to match your risk outcome.

WHAT YOU KNOW NOW:

- What Investment Asset Allocation is;
- The main asset classes and what they are invested in.

13

INVESTING OPTIONS

In the last chapter, we looked at Investment Asset Allocation. The next stage is looking at what can sit inside the Asset Allocation.

WHAT IS A FUND?

A fund is an investment used by investors to pool their money together with other investors. You buy the fund and the fund manager then selects the underlying shares and holdings which the fund buys and invests in.

There are over 9,000 funds globally to pick from, which is a lot of choice; and they are all slightly different.

WHAT IS A SHARE?

A share is a piece of ownership in one company.

Picking the funds to go inside your investment portfolio can be a bit of daunting task. Fortunately, there are many options out there where someone has already done the work for you. I'm going to talk about the options available to you, without having to go through the work of picking your own funds – personally I think letting an expert to do this is the best way forward.

MULTI-MANAGER FUNDS

A multi-manager fund is a fund that is run by a professional fund manager. It invests in a selection of other funds and fund managers to give a diversified portfolio. Multi-manager funds are essentially a one-stop-shop for investors.

There are two kinds of multi-manager funds – fund of funds, and manager of managers.

A fund of funds portfolio holds a selection of funds run by other managers.

A manager of manager portfolio is when the overall manager selects a group of managers who are experts in their field, and they select the funds to invest in. The overall manager monitors the managers and their performance.

Some multi-manager funds are Actively Managed. With actively managed funds, the fund manager is looking at the fund and reviewing, buying and selling funds and actively watching the markets to try and outperform them.

Multi-manager funds are great to give you a diversified portfolio with many options now being risk rated to best match your attitude to risk too.

TRACKER FUNDS

Another popular fund choice is to invest in a Tracker fund. These are considered a passive style of investing.

Passive investing means that the fund is designed to track an index, and the manager behind the fund will just follow what the index is doing.

Different stock markets have different indexes, for example the UK stock market has the FTSE 100 index which is made up of the 100 biggest UK companies. There is also the FTSE 250 index, which is the 250 biggest UK companies after the FTSE 100.

One of the best-known indexes is the S&P 500 Index, or the Standard and Poors 500 Index, which is made up of the largest 500 companies on the American stock markets.

An example of a tracker fund would be a fund which tracks the FTSE 100. The fund will invest in FTSE 100 companies and if you compare the performance of the FTSE 100, the tracker fund should neatly follow this.

SINGLE COMPANY SHARES

A different option is single company shares, however it's important to remember these are higher risk than funds. By selecting individual shares, you won't have the diversification of a fund investing in lots of shares.

If you decided to invest in individual shares, it's important to remember it will be down to you to check on how each company is doing.

I have clients who invest in shares where there is a benefit for them doing so, for example some cruise companies will give a discount on a cruise if you can prove you own shares with them. Adnams for example, also offer a shareholder's discount.

ONLINE INVESTMENT SOLUTIONS

A lot of investment solutions that you can find online give you a choice of portfolios which are related to your attitude to investment risk. You can access a lot of these without the need for a financial adviser.

Sustainable investing is becoming more and more popular, but what is Sustainable Investing?

There are so many words and phrases used to describe what I am referring to as sustainable investing, some of which you may well have come across, including Ethical Investing and Socially Responsible Investing (SRI).

The first sustainable fund was launched in 1984. At the time, it was dubbed the 'Brazil fund'. This wasn't because of the concern for rainforests in Brazil, it was because at the time people joked that you had to be 'nuts' to invest in it. Oh, how things have changed!

Until recently, investing in sustainable funds was usually met at the cost of growth. Many people felt that by choosing to invest sustainably you would be sacrificing the potential of your returns. However, as sustainability has become more important and more popular, this is no longer the case and these funds have started to appear in mainstream portfolios.

But what makes a fund sustainable? At time of writing there isn't a sustainable accreditation which makes a fund easily identifiable as sustainable, but I think that will be coming soon.

Traditionally, investing ethically would mean looking at not investing in companies or funds that invest in certain areas, such as porn, armaments and tobacco; the selection was carried out through a negative screening process. Today however, selecting sustainable companies and funds is done using a much more positive screening process.

There is a set of three standards which are used to measure and evaluate a company's corporate behaviours and their social impact. These are known as ESG, which stands for Environmental Social Governance.

Environmental considers things like energy consumption, pollution, recycling and waste management, natural resource conservation, disposal of hazardous waste and compliance with government environmental regulations.

Social refers to how a company manages its relationships with employees, suppliers, customers and the communities it operates within. It looks at whether the suppliers they use have the same values as them, whether they donate money to support causes in the local community and whether they show a high regard for their employees' health, safety and welfare.

Governance deals with the company's leadership, executive pay, audits, internal controls and shareholder rights. Investors want to know that accurate transparent accounting methods are used, stockholders are being given the opportunity to vote on important issues and avoid conflicts of interest within its board members.

Companies don't have to comply with all of these areas to be considered 'ESG' so it's important to bear that in mind, if you're "sustainably minded".

WHAT YOU KNOW NOW:

- The difference between a fund and a share;
- What a multi manager fund is;
- What a tracker fund is;
- The risk related to single company shares;
- What sustainable investing is.

14

LONG TERM PLANNING OPTIONS

We have talked a lot about short-term goals and short-term saving options; however, I believe there is a reason that we all work long hours and put our heart and soul into our businesses.

Yes, I'm sure you love what you do and you love the impact you have on your clients' lives, whether you have a service based or a product-based business. But essentially, you are working towards your retirement.

What "retirement" may look like for you could be completely different for someone else.

You might be looking forward to the time when you can put your feet up, look back on your achievements, and enjoy life without worrying about work and where the money to pay the bills for your lifestyle is going to come from.

Or you might just what that peace of mind that you can now concentrate on your life goals, with the worry of where your income is coming from.

Whatever it looks like it, know there is no "one size fits all" solution to reaching that retirement. Every one of you is different, and that means that the planning needed will be different to the person next to you, even if that person has a similar business to you.

This is the area that I am most passionate about. I carried out some research with a group of female business owners and entrepreneurs to establish their views on planning for their retirement.

57% of the women who answered knew they needed to plan for their retirement but haven't yet made the time to do it.

9% questioned answered: Retirement? What's that, and 2% thought they were too young to think about retirement.

However, good news, 16% had their retirement all planned out, and were on target for a great one.

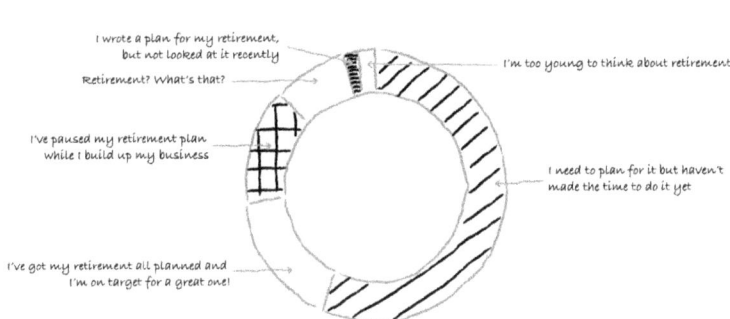

What are your plans for retirement?

I wrote a plan for my retirement, but not looked at it recently

Retirement? What's that?

I've paused my retirement plan while I build up my business

I've got my retirement all planned and I'm on target for a great one!

I'm too young to think about retirement

I need to plan for it but haven't made the time to do it yet

Unfortunately, the results were what I was expecting from the time I have been working in the online space.

You need to take time to create a plan to have something to work towards. Calculating how much you will need to have invested or saved when you reach retirement can be complicated, so, it's easy to put it all off.

Hopefully working through this book will be helping you begin to make those plans and calculations. But there are also a couple of rules that can help when it comes to calculating what you need for retirement.

4% RULE

The 4% rule was developed in 1994 by a financial planner William Bengen in America. He was trying to establish a safe rate of withdrawal which would mean that the money for retirement wouldn't run out. He did a lot of research on data over the 50-year period, from 1926 to 1976, and came up with the 4% rule. Before we continue, there is no guarantee that this will work, however it will give you a number to work with.

The 4% rule is a way to figure out how much your total retirement investments will need to be. The rule of thumb means you should be able to draw out 4% of your assets each year to create your retirement income. For example, if you had £1,000,000 in investments for retirement, drawing 4% per year would give you an annual income of £40,000.

25 X RULE

The 25 x rule works in the opposite way to the 4% rule: if you know the annual income you want at retirement, you can use this to calculate how much you need in the pot at retirement to achieve that.

Simply put, your retirement pot should 25 x your target retirement income. For example, if you target annual retirement income was £50,000, you would want to have a total retirement pot of £1,250,000.

These rules are both rough estimates, but will help give an idea of what to work towards.

SOURCES OF RETIREMENT INCOME

The three most common sources of income in retirement are pensions and investments, property, and your business. The next three chapters look into each of these areas in more detail.

Your retirement doesn't have to be just one of these; it could well be a combination of all three. There may be other ways of funding your retirement in addition to these three, too – a part-time job, for example. Just because you're retiring, it doesn't mean that you won't want to do something else as well – either staying on part-time, doing something similar, or something completely different.

I have friends who have retired but have missed having a purpose and have gone and got themselves part time jobs, volunteering with their favourite charities. Some of them now work in a charity shop, or do conservation work, counting bats in a National Trust for Scotland property.

Personally, I love books and have always wanted to volunteer in a local National Trust property library sorting their books into genres and alphabetically by author. In my spare time currently, I am the chairman of the St Kilda Club, which is a charity that raises awareness and funds for St Kilda, the UK's only dual UNESCO World Heritage site. When I retire, I would love to do more with this, and spend time on St Kilda. I certainly won't be bored!

You may decide to stage your retirement, which could mean working part time at 60, and then retiring fully at age 65, or perhaps even younger.

I have friends who retired at 50, and are living the dream with regular holidays and have lots of interests in the village they live in.

Not that we should try and keep up with the Jones' – everyone's retirement plan is personal to them!

- How to calculate the amount you need in retirement;
- The three main types of retirement income;
- Retirement can look different for everyone.

15

INVESTING FOR YOUR RETIREMENT

I'm excited to write this chapter! Having worked in financial services since I was 21, I have known about pensions and investing in stocks and shares products for a long time, and have seen the benefits they have brought to many clients over the years.

The work we have done on risk, loss and asset allocation has all been leading to this point.

Let's start with pensions.

WHAT IS A PENSION?

Essentially a pension scheme is a type of savings plan to help you save money for your later life – retirement. They have favourable tax treatments compared to other forms of savings. They also lock your money away until you reach a certain age (currently 55, but it has been announced that this will increasing to 57).

I have had a healthy respect for pensions for a long time, and recently I was quite horrified to discover what a poor opinion many people have of them. A lot of this is down to misconceptions, so I'm going to try and answer some of those misconceptions here:

- I don't like personal pensions because of Maxwell...
- I know lots of people who have lost all their money investing in pensions.
- If I have a pension that means I will have failed in my business.
- Pensions won't exist for much longer.
- The State Pension is enough to live off.
- I have no control over what my pension is invested in.
- My retirement plan is just about me.
- I'll worry about my pension later in life.

So, let's start with Maxwell – for those who don't know, this was one of the greatest frauds (and not in a good way) in history. Robert Maxwell owned the Daily Mirror Group, amongst other companies, and he ran up huge debts. To cover it up he took money from one company to give it to another – taking from Peter to pay Paul. When that didn't work, he raided the money from the Mirror Group pension fund.

When he mysteriously died in 1991, the full extent of his activities came to light: he had stolen £450,000,000 from the pension fund. The government did step in and did a partial bailout, however most people ended up with only around 50% of the pension that they should have had.

Two things here: this was a company pension scheme, and not a personal pension, and in the 30 years since there have been many changes to pension regulations, including a pension regulatory body being set up in 1995 to oversee company pension schemes.

I know lots of people who have lost all their money investing in pensions.

With a bit of secondary probing, this comment related to elderly relatives many years ago who used their pension monies to buy what is called an annuity.

When you buy an annuity, you give the provider an amount of money, and for that money, they guarantee to pay you a set amount of money each month for the rest of your life. The problem is that if you die shortly after you buy the annuity then that's it. There is no way to get the money you paid back.

In April 2015, the government announced what is called "Pension Freedoms". This means that rather than buying an annuity, you have the option to take money from your pension as and when you like after reaching the government pension age. There are many benefits to this which I will cover later in the chapter, but one of these is that you don't have to use all the money to buy an annuity, so if you do die shortly after retirement, the value of the pension can be left to your family, and isn't lost.

If I have a pension that means I will have failed in my business.

This one all comes down to mindset. The thought behind this is, if I have to use a pension in retirement, then I won't be a success in my business. But a pension is an amazing tool to use within your business right now. It can be used to help save money on your Corporation Tax bill and it's being saved for you to have access to when you don't want to work anymore.

If you don't need the money from your pension to have an amazing life in retirement, the best bit is by not touching your pension, it will pass to your family, and if you have an Inheritance Tax liability (a topic for another day), then your pension money will fall outside your estate for Inheritance Tax purposes.

Pensions won't exist much longer.

This comment came from a discussion on Clubhouse, and again, after some secondary probing, it became clear they were referring to state pension. Now, I can't say what the government will do with the state pension, or whether it will still exist when you reach 67 or 68 or whatever your government retirement age is as you read this.

Personally, I believe it will exist in some form, but whether it would provide a reasonable income in retirement remains to be seen.

A friend of mine is due to retire shortly and her goal is to see how many bottles of gin she can buy with her first state pension payment! I guess it will depend whether she goes for supermarket own brand, or if she goes for some of the bespoke gins that are so popular now.

Personal Pensions are very much still in existence, as are company pension schemes. With the introduction of Auto Enrolment schemes, it seems the government is definitely pro these rather than against.

THE STATE PENSION IS ENOUGH TO LIVE OFF.

As I've said above, what the future for the State Pension is we just don't know.

However, as it currently stands, for many of us this will not be a significant portion of our retirement income. It definitely shouldn't be the only retirement planning you have in place.

I have no control over what my pension is invested in.

In the good old days, it was possible to buy a lot of different things with your pension. Not always a good thing, but you could buy wine, art or (my personal favourite) tractors and combine harvesters. However, things have changed and there is a limit on what can be bought through a pension today.

It is possible to own commercial property through your pension, and there are lots of funds and shares that can be bought through your pension. In some ways, too much choice can be overwhelming.

MY RETIREMENT PLAN IS JUST ABOUT ME.

Many people believe that their pension pot is just for them, and that they and their partner need to pursue individual retirement strategies.

Now, there is some truth to this one – even with a married couple, each individual's finances will be different, so there can be a level of individualisation to the strategies.

However, your partner *can* inherit your pension pot when you die. Usually, if you're under 75, they'll inherit it tax free, and if you're over 75 they'll only pay tax at their marginal rate.

So, you can take a collective approach to your retirement strategy, the same as you would for any other financial plan.

I'LL WORRY ABOUT MY PENSION LATER IN LIFE.

Probably the most common retirement myth is this one: that there's always time in the future to set up your retirement strategy.

While it's true, and you can always put off sorting out your retirement plans until tomorrow, it's also an extremely harmful myth that can really hurt people's ability to save properly for later life.

The earlier you start saving, the better off you'll be. Even putting a small amount away when you're younger will set you in far better stead later on, through the magic of compound interest.

You're far better off getting your pension sorted early and letting your money work for you over the course of your career!

So, that's all the myth busting done; let's look at pensions in a bit more detail.

PENSIONS' TAX EFFICIENCY

The thing that is so great about pensions is their tax efficiency. Any contributions that you pay personally into your pension will benefit from tax relief.

Tax relief is basically the government giving you money for saving money. The amount of tax you pay will dictate how much you get, but if you are a basic rate tax payer, the government will pay tax relief of 20%.

If you have a limited company, contributing to a pension has significant tax advantages. Pension contributions can be treated as an allowable business expense and offset against your company's corporation tax bill.

PENSION LIMITS

Hopefully by now you will be able to see the benefits of having a pension. But there have to be limits, and this comes in the form of how much you can invest into a pension within any single tax year.

There is an annual allowance amount which limits the amount you can pay into your pension. Also, if you have no earnings, there is a limit in these circumstances too. There is also a lifetime allowance which limits the amount you can have in your pension. You can have more, but there is additional tax to pay on this.

Check out the gov.uk website for the most up-to-date pension allowance figures.

PENSIONS AT RETIREMENT

We have talked about the benefits of paying into a pension, and hopefully dispelled some of those myths about pensions, but what happens at retirement?

We have already established that you can't get your hands on your pension money until 55 (subject to change), so if you are looking to retire earlier than 55, you will need to have something else in place – which we will cover in a moment.

When you decide to take money from your pension, you are currently allowed to take 25% of your pension pot as a tax-free lump sum. Sounds great, doesn't it? But it's important to think whether you are just taking that 25% because it's there, or is it because you need it?

It may be better to take the tax-free cash as income over a period of time. This is where sitting down and working out the most tax efficient way to take your income is really important.

OTHER TAX EFFICIENT RETIREMENT OPTIONS

Another option for long-term investing is paying into an ISA. It doesn't have the tax advantages that a pension has but it is tax free, which means that when you go to take money from your ISA there will be no tax to pay.

Your ISA can even sometimes be invested in the same funds as your pension, or different – it is completely personal to you.

If you only had pensions and ISAs to rely on to provide your income in retirement, it's still important to work out what product you should take the money from each month.

Rule of thumb would be to use the ISA first, however, depending on your tax situation then it could well be a combination of both. If you are retiring before you are able to receive your state pension, this will also have an impact on your choice.

WHAT YOU KNOW NOW:

- The truth behind some of the most popular pension myths;
- Pensions and their tax efficiency;
- What happens when you start taking your pension;
- What other tax efficient retirement planning strategies are out there.

16

PROPERTY

Using property as part of your retirement planning is very popular, and certainly the lure of physically owning something tangible is attractive to many people.

However, as with any kind of investing, it's really important to go into property investing with your eyes wide open and make sure you understand fully what you are getting into.

You may discover that you become an accidental landlord. I know this is something that happened to me. When I met my husband, he initially moved into my house with me along with his large collection of clothes. When he boarded out my loft space and added a proper loft ladder, then proceeded to put my clothes up there, I knew it was time to find a slightly larger house to live in.

We decided to buy our new home first, and then sell my house. However, this was in 2008, and as we completed on our new home in the July, property prices crashed and I made the decision to not sell my house at the time but to rent it out instead. It was a very quick learning curve on all the requirements for renting out a property.

Unless you are an accidental landlord, it is important to do as much research as possible before buying a property to rent. Property can be a good investment, but if you get it wrong, it can also be a very expensive mistake.

Some things to consider include:

Regulations – there are so many different regulations that apply to being a landlord, and they are changing all the time. It's important to fully understand your responsibilities.

How much rental income are you expecting – do some research on similar properties and be realistic – it's better to know upfront rather than finding out later that you have over-estimated.

Ongoing Costs – don't forget that there will be maintenance costs, insurances, safety certificates and more that you will need to pay for in addition.

Do your numbers stack up? – it's really important to get all your ducks in a row, before you even start.

Mortgage lender permission – if you are looking to rent out an existing property that you own, make sure you check you have permission from your mortgage lender to do this. It may need changing to a buy to let mortgage, or they may give you a special permission for a period of time.

Tax implications – there is lots of different tax implications with renting out a property, make sure you are up to date on all the different rules

Managing your property – will you do this yourself, or are you planning on using a property management company? What are the costs for each option? Do you have the time to manage it yourself?

Finding the right tenant – make sure you do your due diligence on your potential tenants, check their credit history, and don't be afraid to turn someone down

As you can see, buying the property is only a small part of having property as an investment.

The other really important factor is liquidity; how are you planning on using your property in your retirement?

Is it your plan to sell the property, or properties, to release capital to fund your retirement? Or are you planning on using the rental income as part of your income in retirement? What happens if you can't sell the property? What happens if the property sits empty? If you are managing the property yourself, will you still want to do this when you are retired? What are the costs of having someone to manage the property for you?

Having a professional to help with this, especially if it's your first journey into investing in property, is something I would highly recommend.

At the time of going to print, the details in this chapter were correct. However, the government guidelines on property are changing all the time, please make sure to check for the most up to date information.

WHAT YOU KNOW NOW:

- The pros and cons of owning property investments;
- Things to consider when renting out a property.

17

YOUR BUSINESS

Many of us work for years and years, growing and nurturing our businesses, almost like it's our child. But what is going to happen when you want to stop working? What's going to happen to your business? Have you thought about it?

Are you relying on selling your business to fund your retirement? Do you know what your business is worth? Have you built a legacy business? Do you have a succession plan in place?

So many questions, so many things to think about, but it's important to start planning as early as possible.

For my business, I made the decision that I wanted to leave behind a legacy, I didn't want the company to just come to an end when I decide to retire. For one, we have clients who rely on us, and I feel a moral obligation to do the right thing and to make sure my departure from the company will be as smooth a transition as possible for everyone.

I started putting plans in place almost 10 years ago, and as the time has passed, I have honed what needs to be put in place, making sure I have the right team to carry on the company when I'm enjoying myself travelling the world – or whatever it is that I will be doing!

However, if you are looking to sell your business, do you know what your business is worth? What exactly are you selling?

You may have a commercial property that your business owns, or your pension may own it – will you be looking to continue getting rent, or will your pension sell the property to the new buyers?

What if you are your business? YOU being your brand is very popular at the moment, but how does that look when you decide to hand the reins to someone else? What are people buying? You want out, so it won't be you!

Having a chat with an expert in this field early on is important. They will be able to tell you the truth as it is and advise on what steps will make the business worth more when you do want to sell.

How long does it take to sell a business? If you have a date in mind for retirement, don't leave things to the last minute, make sure you leave time for the process.

How do you want to be paid? This applies to selling your business, or if you have built a team to take over from you. It's not usual to receive a lump sum all upfront, it is usually over a period of time, with caveats in place if growth isn't as expected, which may mean you receive less than you expect.

What if your family is involved with the business? I have a client who grew a successful business with the view that when they got to retirement it would be sold, and that would form part of their retirement. However, their children work in the business, and want to continue running it. Could this be you?

Whatever your plans for your business – legacy or selling, here are some things that you can be thinking about now...

TAKING MONEY FROM THE BUSINESS BEFORE RETIREMENT

Taking money from your business in the form of pension contributions is great for not just getting cash out of the business, but also reducing any corporation tax liability.

Speak to an accountant about how you take income from your business to make sure you are being as tax efficient as possible. They will be able to advise on the amount of PAYE to take and dividend payments.

MAKING YOUR BUSINESS EXIT READY:

- Make sure your business isn't reliant on you. I know someone who has a team meeting once a month, and each month they review whether or not it would be possible to fire them – this is a great way of looking at it as you get ready to exit.
- Make sure the legal structure of the business is right.
- Get the right team in place – if you haven't done already, look to recruit for the right people. Don't be afraid to make hard decisions. You are planning for your future, not anyone else's!

When you have a plan in place, and a buyer or the team to take over, make sure you seek legal and financial advice to ensure that you benefit from the different tax advantages that are available to you.

- Your options when leaving your business;
- What you can do now with your business to help fund your retirement;
- How to make your business exit ready.

REVIEW, REWRITE, REPEAT

Through this book we have covered the ways for you to be financially savvy.

We have talked about understanding your Money Mindset, how to make changes to improve your Money Mindset and how to deal with money blocks.

We have delved into Knowing your Finances, going through everything you already have in place, making sure you know everything there is, the values of long forgotten savings plans and investment and pension statements.

We went through what your Financial Focus is, what your goals for the future are, be those short-term or long-term.

And then we set your course and put together the plan for you to start working towards achieving those goals.

Now we come to perhaps the most important stage when it comes to planning for your future, especially your longer term goals and plans, and that is to review the plans and goals you have put in place.

WHY IS REVIEWING SO IMPORTANT?

Whatever your goals are, you need to check back to see what has happened since you originally sat down and established them and put your plan in place.

What has changed? Your circumstances? Your priorities? Even your goals?

You may have wanted to retire at 50, but actually you now really love what you are doing and can imagine doing it for longer. Perhaps you are now considering going part time at 50, and not fully retiring until 60. This will impact how much money you will want to have put away for your retirement.

For your short-term goals, for example, you may feel you don't want to go abroad this year, but stay in the UK for your holidays, this may give you longer to reach that holiday goal you had put in place.

You may decide that the windows really do need replacing sooner rather than later, so that priority needs moving up the list, or perhaps your car didn't have the best MOT visit, and it may need replacing sooner than you had planned.

It could be that there has been a change in your finances affecting the money coming into the home. Maybe there is a work or a personal issue that throws your plans into disarray. You may feel that you just want to curl up in a ball. But don't panic, try and look forward and make a new plan and set new goals if applicable.

Life throws many challenges at us, and a lot of those will have a financial impact on the plans we have in place.

Reviewing doesn't just mean looking at your goals, but also where you are at with your planning. Have you stuck to your plan? Have you remembered to move the money across to your different savings pots each month? Are your savings at the levels you were expecting them to be at?

Have you slipped off the wagon and started buying that coffee each morning again? If you are on track, are you making sure you are putting the money away that you would have spent? This may seem obvious, but I followed a money group in America, and the coffee saving tip is a popular one. One member of the group had not been buying the daily coffee but she also hadn't been putting the money aside, and her question was, where's the money gone? Of course, as it had stayed in her purse or bank account, she had spent it on something else!

I would also suggest re-looking at your bank statement when you review. Things that you subscribe to that were important to you at your initial plan stage may have changed.

I saw a new client recently. She had hit her goals and was feeling like a fish out of water – what was next? She had missed the most important stage along her journey: reviewing where she was at, and not revisiting her goals and updating them as her circumstances changed. We sat down and she established new goals and plans, and left feeling much more focused.

With savings, I would suggest having a look once a month to see how things are looking, with perhaps a sit down to look at your goals on a quarterly basis.

With investments I would recommend not looking as regularly as they are set up for your long-term goals and may move up and down with the volatility of the market. Looking too often may worry you unnecessarily.

If you have done your investments through a professional, you will find that they will arrange a meeting with you on an annual or a six-monthly basis. I would wait for this meeting and review your investments with your professional.

If you have done them yourselves, I would say looking every quarter should be enough, but please don't worry if they seem to go up and down, that can be perfectly normal.

A good plan for the future is flexible; reviewing it will help you realise when you need to make changes to any part of it.

Review, rewrite and repeat!

WHAT YOU KNOW NOW:

- Why reviewing is important;
- What you should be reviewing and how often;
- How to learn to enjoy the process.

19

SAFETY NETS – PROTECTION

Being financially savvy isn't just about knowing your finances, having realistic goals and have a regularly reviewed plan. It's also about understanding the importance of what I like to call the safety nets, for when things don't go to plan.

In this chapter, we're going to be looking at protection: what it means, why it's important and what you should have in place, depending on your circumstances.

"Life Insurance – in case you can't be there to catch them, make sure you leave a safety net."

Statistics from Scottish Widows latest protection research show that "8.2 million UK homeowners have no life cover in place" and "only 20% of UK homeowners who have life cover, have critical illness cover in place", this is such an important topic, and an area that I would recommend everyone looking at.

WHAT IS LIFE COVER?

Life cover describes a selection of different products, but essentially it is a policy that will pay out money in the event of the death of the policy owner.

It is usually taken out when you buy a house, to cover a mortgage debt. There are two types of plan depending on the type of mortgage you have.

Most people today have repayment mortgages. This is when each monthly payment pays off the monthly interest and an element of the capital debt too, so that the mortgage amount owed decreases the more payments are made.

With this type of mortgage, the life cover to go with it is called Decreasing Term Assurance, and as the name would suggest, the amount of cover decreases in line with your mortgage.

For example, a Decreasing Term Assurance policy is taken out for £200,000 to cover the cost of a repayment mortgage of £200,000. After 12 months, the amount owing on the mortgage is £188,000. The amount of cover you have available with the Decreasing Term Assurance will decrease each year to match this.

The other type of mortgage is an Interest Only mortgage. This is where each month you are only paying off the interest, and at the end of the mortgage term you will still owe the same amount as you borrowed at the start of the mortgage.

With this type of mortgage, the life cover to go with this is called Level Term Assurance, and the cover stays the same for the whole term of the mortgage, and in the event of death, the whole mortgage amount would be paid off.

For example, a Level Term Assurance policy is taken out for £200,000 over 20 years to cover the cost of an interest only mortgage of £200,000. The term of the mortgage is 20 years. After 20 years you will still owe £200,000. The amount of cover you have available with the Level Term Assurance will same at £200,000 for the term of the plan.

If you live alone, then there isn't really a need for life cover as the property could be sold after you have died to pay off the mortgage. However, a different type of cover that is worth considering in all the circumstances above, whether you are single or living with a partner, with or without children, is Critical Illness Cover.

WHAT IS CRITICAL ILLNESS COVER?

Critical Illness cover can be a standalone product, but it is usually an addition to a life cover plan.

Whereas life cover only pays out in the event of the death of the life which the plan covers, Critical illness cover will pay out in the event of that person being diagnosed with a critical illness.

There are different providers that can offer Critical Illness cover, and each covers a variety of different illnesses, however, they all usually all cover what is known as "the big three" in the industry:

- Cancer
- Heart Attacks
- Strokes.

With the mortgage gone, your monthly outgoings will be significantly reduced, but what happens to your family if one of you isn't there anymore, or you are still there as a mouth to feed, and also need someone to look after you?

To help calculate the level of cover you need, one suggestion is to multiply your income by three, and add this amount as the critical illness element of your plan, this would mean that you would still receive a lump sum equivalent to three years income.

One option is to increase the amount of life cover you have so there is more for your family, or alternatively, there is a product called Family Income Benefit.

FAMILY INCOME BENEFIT

Family Income Benefit is the cheapest form of life cover. These plans are usually used when there is a young family, and they end when the youngest child reaches 18 or 21. Calculate how much annual income your family would need in the event of your or your partners' death to help calculate the level of cover you need.

The plan will pay out a monthly or quarterly payment until the end date of the policy, from the date of death. It is cheaper than other types of life cover as it will only pay out for the term left, and the longer than plan runs, the less it will pay out.

For a couple with a young family with a mortgage, to have a combination of a life and critical illness plan and a Family Income Benefit plan is a good plan to have in place.

TERMINAL DEATH BENEFIT

The majority of life cover plans include a Terminal Death Benefit. This is different to Critical Illness; it means that in the event of being diagnosed with a terminal illness, and being given less than a year to live, the product provider will pay out the amount of cover early.

One question I get asked a lot is, is there a value to the plans when they end? And the answer is: unfortunately, not. These plans are purely for protection. If we could look in a crystal ball and see when our loved one's would die then there would be no need for these types of plans; unfortunately, we can't.

Another important point to remember is that when you move house or re-mortgage, you must make sure that your life cover is still relevant and provides you with the right cover. Normally, when we move or re-mortgage there is some change made, an increase in cover, a change in term – if your life cover is in place to cover your mortgage, it's important to review at the same time.

WORK BASED DEATH IN SERVICE COVER

For those of you where you or your partner works for a large corporate or public sector employer, there is usually a death in service plan which will pay out a percentage of your salary on your death. But remember, if you change job, then this cover will no longer apply.

WHAT YOU KNOW NOW:

- What life cover is and why it's important;
- The types of life cover and the difference between them.

20

SAFETY NETS – INCOME PROTECTION

Let's get the scary statistics out of the way first. Every year at least a million people are unable to work because of a serious illness or injury.

Before we dive into the different types of Income Protection, too many times do I see people dismissing Income Protection, as they don't believe they will be ill enough to ever have to use the cover - if they break a leg, then they can work from home. However, no one knows what the future may hold, and it will not only cover those visible illnesses, but also the not so visible, mental health conditions

There are two types of Income Protection, a short-term version and a long-term option. As you can imagine, the short-term option tends to be a lot cheaper than the long-term.

Let's look at the long-term version first.

INCOME PROTECTION

Essentially Income Protection does what it says on the tin, it protects your income in the event of you being unable to work. It is suitable for you if you live alone, or if you have a family.

So, why have it? With all protections, this is one that you hope you will never need to claim on. You may see this as dead money, but imagine what your life would look like if you don't have the cover in place, and you can't work because of ill health?

Before taking out cover, it's important to see if you have benefits in place from any employment, and to look and see what the government benefits would be in the event of you being unable to work due to a serious illness or injury.

It's important to make sure you have the correct amount of cover; if you are over insured, when it comes to claiming, the plan provider will want evidence of your earnings at that time, and only pay up to the percentage that they have agreed to cover. Most providers pay out between 60-75% of your income (providing you have that much cover in place).

Another important consideration is when you want payments to start – the longer you can leave it before you can claim, the cheaper the premium. They call these a deferred period – from the date you have been diagnosed, you can set a deferred period for when your cover will start. This can be from four weeks, up to 52 weeks.

If you have an employer who pays full pay for 26 weeks, then half pay for the next 26 weeks, then stops, you can set up a plan, which pays out half the income after 26 weeks, and then the full amount after 52 weeks.

Usually, Income Protection plans are designed to finish when you plan to retire, and you can set that date when you start the policy.

When you return to work, your cover is still there, in the event that you need to claim on it again, and the premiums will not be impacted by your time when you were claiming.

The majority of illnesses are covered by Income Protection plans, however it's always important to read the details of the plan, to make sure you don't get any surprises.

How does this differ from Critical Illness?

With Critical Illness cover, you receive a lump sum pay-out in the event of being diagnosed with a Critical Illness. With Income Protection, if you are unable to work because of a serious illness or injury, you will receive a monthly income after a pre-determined period of time.

If your Critical Illness cover only covers your mortgage, then it won't take into account any other bills.

The two covers complement each other, to provide a comprehensive protection for you and your family.

SHORT TERM INCOME PROTECTION

Short Term Income Protection is designed to pay out for a short period of time, usually between one and two years. They can pay out on redundancy (although this are much rarer to find these days), an accident or sickness. They are designed to cover mortgage payments for a short period of time.

They are a lot cheaper than the Income Protection plans, however their benefits are a lot less. Along with the much shorter term, you will be limited on the circumstances that they will pay out for.

Redundancy won't be covered if the work is seasonal or voluntary, and not all illnesses will be covered, so it's really important to check the wording before taking out any cover.

There will also be a period of time before you will receive any money, which will usually be 30 days.

With the Protections covered here, you may decide that you can't afford the cover, or that they aren't appropriate for you. However, it's really important to be aware of the different options available and obtain quotes, so you are aware of the costs and the cover you could have.

When applying for any cover, there will be medical questions asked. It's important to always answer them as fully as possible. Although the providers of protection have a good track record of paying out for cover, if you have failed to mention something which you then try to claim for later on, they will reject your claim.

WHAT YOU KNOW NOW:

- What Income Protection covers;
- The differences between the types of cover and how each works.

SAFETY NETS – WRITING A WILL

Did you know:

- 5.4 million adults do not know where to begin when it comes to writing a will
- Around 54% of adults do not have a will
- Six in 10 (59%) parents do not have a will, or have one that is out of date.

*Statistics from Royal London Annual Report

How many times have you thought about writing a will, only to put it to the side for later and promptly forgotten all about it? You are not alone!

Writing a will is one of those things that many of us know we really should do. But life is busy, so it tends to get pushed to the bottom of the pile. Having a will is so important though, especially if you have children.

WHAT IS A WILL?

Your will is essentially a set of instructions that dictate how the things you leave behind should be shared out. It's the only legally binding way for making sure your wishes are followed once you pass away.

Having a will gives you the power to make sure your money, property and possessions go to the people you intend. It can also let your family know of any other wishes you may have, such as plans for your funeral.

Here are five more very good reasons why getting your will ticked off the to do list is a must.

1. **You get to decide who gets what when you die.** This is especially important if you're not married or in a civil partnership. Or, if you want include someone who is not in your immediate family. Without a will, the courts will decide what to do with all your belongings. They may not share out your estate in a way you would like.
2. **You can make sure your children (under the age of 18) are looked after.** Within a will you're able to appoint a guardian for your children should you die whilst they still need caring for. If you don't have a will, the court will choose among your family members or a state-appointed guardian.
3. **It saves your loved ones a lot of trouble.** If all your wishes are written down in black and white, there's much less chance of disagreement and upset.
4. **It avoids a lengthy probate process.** Most estates must go through probate. Having a will speeds up the process meaning any beneficiaries have access to their share sooner.
5. **A will can reduce the amount of Inheritance Tax.** With a

bit of planning, more of what you have worked hard for will go where you want it, rather than being paid out in taxes.

THINGS TO CONSIDER WHEN WRITING YOUR WILL

Making a will can be a bit of an undertaking. There is a lot to consider. It's important to take time to plan. Knowing exactly what you have and where you would like it to go will make the writing of your will much easier.

Below is a guide as to the sort of details a will writer would need from you:

- **Marriage:** Date and place of marriage or civil partnership. Details of any previous marriages, including children of a previous marriage. A copy of your marriage certificate/civil partnership certificate may be useful to keep stored with your will.
- **Children:** Full names of all children, their dates of birth and current addresses (if different from yours).
- **Guardians for children:** Full names and addresses of guardians to be appointed to look after minor children (under the age of 18).
- **Executors:** Full names and addresses of executors to deal with the winding up of your estate. They may also become trustees if applicable.
- **Gifts:** Details of any specific gifts (including charitable gifts) you wish to make in your will. These should include full names and addresses of the recipients.
- **The residue of your estate:** An indication of how you wish the residue (i.e., the balance of the estate after gifts and liabilities are settled) to be distributed.
- In the case of a married couple, the residue is usually left to each other. Thereafter, it is normally divided equally

between children when they reach a specified age (minimum 18).

- **Minors:** Where there are minor children, the will should contain powers for executors to invest capital in anything they consider to be for the benefit of the children. It should also contain a power to advance capital to each child under the age at which they inherit.
- **Pets:** If you have animals or pets, we recommend that you leave detailed instructions for looking after them. Your will can include financial provision for them if you wish.
- **After death:** If you choose, your will may set out your personal wishes on matters such as burial, cremation, organ donation and medical research.

WHAT ARE DIY WILLS AND ARE THEY LEGALLY VALID?

These days, it's not uncommon to find that someone has written their own will. Templates for DIY wills are readily available and are much cheaper than hiring a professional, making them an appealing option.

But are these self-made wills legal? Will they stand up and do the job when the time comes?

WHAT IS A DIY WILL?

First of all, it makes sense to understand what a DIY will actually is. In very basic terms, a DIY will is one which has been written without the services of a solicitor or will writing professional.

ARE DIY WILLS LEGALLY VALID?

In short, yes. They are valid as long as you have met the legal requirements. For a will to be legal it must be written down and made by a person of sound mind on their own accord. It should be signed in the presence of two witnesses who then also sign and date the document.

In theory, it is entirely possible to jot down your will on to the back of an old envelope. As long as you have signed it in front of two witnesses and those witnesses have signed it in return, it should be legally valid.

Obviously, this is not a recommended method for writing your will! It's best to have something a little more formal. There are templates available online and in some stationery shops which are a better place to start if opting for a self-written will.

SELF-MADE WILLS CAN BE RISKY

One of the main issues with DIY wills is that they can easily be rendered invalid, contain mistakes or accidentally leave out assets. If the proper wording isn't used, they can be left open to interpretation and, therefore, confusion between the executor and beneficiaries.

If it isn't expressly obvious what wishes your will is setting out, claimants could dispute the will. A disputed will can be a lengthy and expensive process. It's stressful for your loved ones and could lead to rifts in the family if a dispute turns particularly nasty. Which is probably not the legacy you want to leave behind, is it?

The legal fees associated with resolving an argument would most likely be paid out of your estate. This would also impact your beneficiaries as reducing the value of your estate would mean reducing the inheritance available for them.

If you don't know what you are doing, you could leave yourself open to misinterpretation. Common mistakes people make when writing their own will include:

- Accidentally leaving out assets and not considering how debts (like a mortgage) could reduce your estate. This could lead to your beneficiaries receiving less than you intend.
- Forgetting to update your will with any change of circumstance, including named executors or beneficiaries dying before you.
- Choosing executors who are unsuitable. For example, someone who is under 18 or lives outside of the UK.
- Trying to amend your will yourself after it has been witnessed and signed. This can only be done with a codicil which is an official alteration. Again, this must be signed and witnessed to be legal.
- Not using the correct wording. For example, not using someone's full name.

In general, the consensus is that DIY wills should be reserved for only very simple situations. For example, a husband and wife who want to leave everything to each other.

Checklist for writing your own will

If you decide that a DIY will is appropriate for you, here are some key things to remember:

- Make sure your will is correctly signed, dated and witnessed.
- Your witnesses cannot benefit from your will, nor be the spouse of someone who will benefit from your will.

- Be specific; rather than leaving your 'property' to someone, write down the full address and rather than leaving everything to your 'husband/wife', use their full name.
- Make sure everything is spelled correctly.
- Destroy any old wills and make sure your new one says that you revoke any previous versions of your will.
- Tell your executor where your will is being kept.

WHEN SHOULD YOU ASK A WILL WRITING PROFESSIONAL TO HELP?

Having seen the fall out when self-made wills go wrong, I would recommend always getting professional help when it comes to will writing. But there are some situations when a self-written will simply isn't appropriate. Life can be complicated and if your will reflects that, you really should seek professional help. Particularly if:

- You have a blended family. This covers separation, divorce and remarriage, step-children or step-siblings;
- You have a dependent who is unable to care for themselves;
- You share a property with someone you're not married to;
- You own a property, shares or bank account overseas;
- You own a business;
- You want to set up a trust;
- You're trying to reduce your IHT bill.

You may think that you have plenty of time to get your will sorted, but you never know what is around the corner. It never hurts to be well prepared and get your affairs in order. The great thing about wills is they can be updated as your situation in life changes.

Having a will and reviewing it regularly is the best way to make sure you are prepared, and your family is looked after, should the worst happen.

REVIEWING YOUR WILL

If you do already have a will, you should check it from time to time to make sure you're still happy with it. If you have an old will, it will be used, even if it's not what your wishes are now. We can help you update an existing will to reflect any changes in your life.

WHAT YOU KNOW NOW:

- What a will is;
- Things to consider when writing your will;
- What a DIY will is, and when it's best to seek professional help.

22

SAFETY NETS – LASTING POWERS OF ATTORNEY

It may seem like you are too young to be worrying about things like Lasting Powers of Attorney. We were talking life cover a couple of chapters back, and supporting a young family, and it may be the case that you are too young to be thinking about getting a Lasting Power of Attorney written. However, this chapter isn't just about you, it's also about the impact an older parent may have on your life.

As a population we live longer, the chances of needed to have something in place is becoming more and more important.

WHAT IS A LASTING POWER OF ATTORNEY (LPA)?

It is a legal document which allows decisions to be made for you, or actions to be completed on your behalf, if you are no longer able to make your own choices.

There are two types of LPA:

Lasting Powers of Attorney for Health and Care Decisions

This type of Lasting Powers of Attorney can only be used when mental capacity has been lost. Decisions made under this LPA might include:

- Where you should live
- The medical care you should receive
- The food you eat and the activities you take part in
- Who contact should be made with.

It might even include special permission for the attorney to make life saving treatment decisions for you.

Lasting Powers of Attorney Financial Decisions

This type of LPA can be used whilst you still have mental capacity. You can state that it comes into force if you lose capacity. The types of things it might cover include:

- Buying and selling property
- Mortgage payments
- Money investments
- Bill payment
- Property repairs.

WHO NEEDS AN LPA?

There may come a day where you or a family member are no longer able to make decisions for yourself or themselves. It's not a pleasant thought but it's entirely possible and it's happening to many people every single day.

The elderly in particular are most likely require the use of an LPA. Dementia is one of the main culprits for leaving individuals unable to make their own decisions. One person develops dementia every three minutes in the UK. According to the Alzheimer's Society, in the UK there is 850,000 people with dementia, with the number likely to rise to 1.6 million by 2040.

Nominating someone to be in charge of your affairs, whilst you still have the ability to do so, goes some way to providing you with peace of mind that you will be looked after as you wish.

WHAT HAPPENS IF THERE IS NO LPA IN PLACE?

In cases where an individual is no longer able to make their own decisions and does not have an LPA in place, your solicitor or a family member will have to apply to the Court of Protection to be appointed as your deputy.

You may not have expressed you wishes to the person who becomes your deputy, which means you may not find yourself in a situation you'd hoped for. Having an LPA in place ensures that you do.

WHAT DOES BEING AN ATTORNEY MEAN?

An LPA is an agreement between a "donor", who is the person you'll make decisions for, and the "attorneys", who make the decisions. There may be several attorneys, and they may have to agree either unanimously on decisions or be able to make them individually.

If you agree to be an attorney under a Lasting Power of Attorney, you'll have a number of responsibilities. These include:

- **Acting in the donor's best interests.** This applies to any decision you make for the donor under an LPA.
- **Ensuring that you act within the terms of the LPA itself.** This means following restrictions and complying with any specific details.

- **Helping the donor make their own decisions.** The expectation of an LPA is that you will not take control unless you have to.

These responsibilities apply to every LPA. However, you should remember that an LPA may change and develop over time. For example, sometimes a donor may only temporarily lack capacity to make decisions. In this case, you may need to make some decisions and then return to helping the donor make them themselves.

WHAT KINDS OF DECISIONS MIGHT YOU HAVE TO MAKE?

The exact decisions you may have to make as an attorney will vary depending on the type of LPA and the specific circumstances of the situation.

The two types of LPAs outlined above may have different attorneys, so if you're appointed under one type and an LPA of the other type is also in force, you'll need to consult with the other attorney on decisions that fall under their remit. For example, if you're under a Health and Welfare LPA and you need to make changes to care plans that cost money, you'll have to discuss this with an attorney for the Property and Financial Affairs LPA.

HOW YOU SHOULD MAKE THESE DECISIONS

Any decision you make in your position as an attorney under an LPA must be made in the donor's best interests. This means you need to think carefully about each decision and consider things like the donor's past wishes.

You should also try and help the donor to make decisions on their own, for example by explaining things simply and giving them time to think. It's best to start from the assumption that the donor can make each decision, rather than taking control.

You should try to avoid making decisions that restrict the donor's human or civil rights as much as is possible. If you do have to make a decision like this, consider if you can do so in a way that is less restrictive but achieves the same purpose.

You can take advice on decisions if you feel that you cannot make them yourself. However, you usually can't delegate responsibility to someone else – you need to make the decision yourself. Some LPAs may specifically offer you this ability, for example if there is a large investment that needs to be managed.

The specific legal principles you must follow when making these decisions

You must follow the principles set out in the Mental Capacity Act 2005 Code of Practice. This document establishes many of the points already discussed in this article but also covers lots more detail. You should ensure you're familiar with it before undertaking your duties as an attorney.

WHAT YOU KNOW NOW:

- The different types of Lasting Power of Attorney;
- Why it's important to have Lasting Powers of Attorney in place;
- What the responsibilities of an attorney are;
- What happens if someone loses capacity and doesn't have Lasting Powers of Attorney in place.

23

WHY PEOPLE USE FINANCIAL ADVISERS

I've worked in the financial services industry for over 20 years, and talking about money and helping people understand their money and finances is something that I'm really passionate about.

It is believed that almost 2 out of 3 people in the UK have never received financial advice which, I have to say, terrifies me.

What we do with our money will have a significant bearing on the life we will lead and future we will have. I'm guessing the majority of us would rather get behind the wheel of a car that's been serviced by someone who really knows what they're doing, but many people don't apply the same logic to servicing their finances.

Recent reports from the International Longevity Centre and Royal London found that speaking to a financial adviser left people better off in both financial assets and in pension wealth.

Having an ongoing relationship with a financial adviser leads to better financial outcomes.

Financial Advisers look at the big picture

Have you been to see a specialist with the issue you think you have, only to leave with a completely different angle on what you felt was the problem, and discover that something else was the issue?

It happens all the time.

Financial Advisers sit down with you, and ask you tons of questions, they get to know your finances, they concentrate on what your Financial Focus is, and help set a course – does any of that sound familiar?

Importantly, they bring a fresh set of eyes and years of experience dealing with other clients' situations and circumstances.

They then go away with the details of your existing plans and pensions, and find out if they are working as hard for you as they should be. With all that information, they will be able to come back to you with a plan and ideas that you might not have considered.

Financial Advisers know about tax and stuff

Financial Advisers have to sit loads of exams and sit through hours of Continued Professional Development every year. They have to understand about tax and all sorts of other complicated things to be able to do the job they do.

To become a Financial Adviser, there's at least two years worth of exams to do, followed by having to be mentored by someone, until they are considered competent to be let loose on the general public. Even then, everything they do is checked by a highly qualified compliance department.

They work alongside your accountants to make tax efficient decisions that they can advise you on, and put it in a language that you will be able to understand.

Understand Your options with good financial advice

In financial services there are lots of different products, I have covered some in this book, but there are lots of different ones out there which may be perfect for you.

It's the financial adviser's job to know the options available to you, and advise on the right options and products for you.

Independent Financial Advisers are regulated

Alongside all those exams and mentoring, before a Financial Adviser is a Financial Adviser they have to be regulated.

In the UK, independent financial advisers (IFAs) are regulated by the Financial Conduct Authority (FCA).

This governing body provides a list of minimum requirements that companies and persons providing financial services must meet to ensure that they are providing a fair and quality service to their clients.

Regulated advisers approved by the FCA must meet minimum qualifications. In order to be approved by the FCA, they must demonstrate their honesty, integrity, competence, capability and knowledge of financial products and services.

The FCA has a register where you can check if someone is regulated by the FCA, it should also be on all their paperwork that you get when you first start working with them. But a good first step is to check out someone's regulatory status.

A Financial Adviser will do the hard work for you

One of the main reasons why people use a financial adviser is to save time. Personally, I'm a strong believer in letting the experts do what they are good at. I don't cut my own hair (although I didn't do a bad job of my husband's in lockdown), I go and see a well-qualified, experienced hairdresser who advises me against those rash decisions of dyeing my hair green!

Financial advisers do all the research and come to you with what they recommend you should do. Using cashflow planning they can show you what your future could look like and how you can achieve your financial goals.

Then they come back on a regular basis to review what you have put in place, and check it still matches your goals and meets your requirements.

WHAT YOU KNOW NOW:

- The benefits of working with an independent financial adviser;
- What a financial adviser will do for you.

24

TIME TO NAVIGATE YOUR OWN JOURNEY

The time has come for my book to finish, but this doesn't mean the end of help and support for you. I hope you have found The Money Compass – the book, informative and that it helped put you on the right path to navigate towards your own financial success.

Please feel free to pop back in and re-read chapters, and please visit my website www.themoneycompass.co.uk/book for all the resources that I have talked about throughout the book, and much more.

I would love to hear about your journey, please feel free to email me at julie@themoneycompass.co.uk or by joining my Facebook group at

www.facebook.com/groups/themoneycompass

Remember that you are not alone on this journey, and there is no such thing as a silly question! I look forward to hearing from you.

NOTES

2. RELATIONSHIPS AND MONEY

1. Conducted by Ramsey Solutions

Lightning Source UK Ltd.
Milton Keynes UK
UKHW022042151121
394037UK00011BA/676/J